Why is **Christianity** Not Widely
Believed in Japan?

Recording the vision. Making it plain. That you may run.

Why is **Christianity** Not Widely
Believed in Japan?

ENDORSEMENTS

Dr. Samuel Lee's most valuable contribution to the theme of *The Japanese & Christianity* is that he emphasizes the qualitative significance of Christianity in Japan more than its quantitative significance. It is also original that Lee integrates the so-called 'political factors' into his assessment of the many other factors that play a role in the Japanese context. That makes the reading of this book an exciting and enriching experience.

Prof. Dr. Martien E. Brinkman
Professor of Intercultural Theology
VU University Amsterdam

Samuel Lee's book *The Japanese and Christianity: Why Is Christianity Not Widely Believed in Japan?* is an ambitious attempt to answer the question that has been raised from many quarters, especially missionary ones. This book is written on the basis of the author's extensive reading of the theme-related works from a wide range of historical, theological, and missiological backgrounds. This book succeeds in crystalizing the conspicuous features of the multifaceted Japanese ideological and spiritual reality. Rightly emphasized are the "wa" principle and corporatism. What I see as the most valuable contribution of this book to the understanding of the theme is the author's emphasis on the qualitative significance of Christianity ("Influence") more than its quantitative, statistical growth in Japan, because the statistic figures betray the true feature of the strong presence of Christianity in Japan.

Dr. Akio Hashimoto
Dean of the Kobe Lutheran Theological Seminary

Christianity's place in Japan has baffled many analysts. How could the world's largest religious movement that was imported several centuries ago, brought by numerous highly motivated emissaries and with a colorful indigenous history, still be so small? Japan's place in world Christianity is similarly enigmatic. It has a widely admired culture and an emulated modernization, yet with resented militaristic periods along with inscrutable international relationships. Where does Japanese Christianity fit within the rest of this worldwide faith? Samuel Lee's study provides an honest, wide-sweeping, and multifaceted look at the complex relationship between Japanese people and Christianity. The practical goal is clarity and constructive relations. I highly commend Lee's helpful analysis.

Rev. J. Nelson Jennings, Ph.D.
Executive Director, Overseas Ministries Study Center
Author of *Theology in Japan: Takakura Tokutaro (1885-1934)*
(University Press of America, 2005).

It can be said that Japan is one of the most difficult countries to evangelize. Many pastors and missionaries are still struggling with the evangelical mission to the Japanese people and trying to find the key to helping them accept the Christian faith. Dr. Samuel Lee bravely challenged this difficult problem. I am very grateful to his profound research, and I sense his genuine love for the Japanese people. I hope and believe that this book will greatly help those who share the gospel to the Japanese people.

Professor Noriyuki Miyake
Academic Dean of Central Bible College
Senior Pastor of Grace Gospel Christ Church in Tokyo
Author of *Belong, Experience, Believe: Pentecostal Mission Strategies for Japan* (Wide Margin, 2005).

The Japanese and Christianity by Dr. Samuel Lee contributes greatly to not only European but also Japanese academia. It definitely opens our eyes to Japanese Christian history, from the encounter of the West to after World War II. The historical, sociological and theological points of view are crucial. At the same time, Lee emphasizes the Japanese worldview. Without a deep understanding of Japanese worldview, it would be difficult to develop a mission work in one of the most challenging countries in the world. We thank Lee for this book that brings together important information for our knowledge of the soil of Japan. I believe it will help future development and bring about dramatic change for a better world.

Professor Toshifumi Uemura,
Director of Christian Programs
Japan Lutheran College, Tokyo

Why is **Christianity** Not Widely
Believed in Japan?

"Sin, he reflected, is not what it is usually thought to be; it is not to steal and tell lies.

Sin is for one man to walk brutally over the life of another and to be quite oblivious of the wounds left behind."

Shusaku Endo, *Silence*

Why is **Christianity** Not Widely
Believed in Japan?

*Dedicated to my **beloved** family,
particularly my parents and my wife.*

Why is **Christianity** Not Widely
Believed in Japan?

ABSTRACT

Since the mid-sixteenth century, Christianity has been notably active in Japan, and yet Japan remains one of the least-evangelized nations in the world. The Japanese and Christianity is an attempt to work out an appropriate response to the question, "What are the main reasons why Christianity has not yet succeeded in Japan?" It investigates various factors, i.e. the societal, cultural, historical, missiological and political dimensions of Christianity in Japan, in searching for possible answers. Generally, Christianity's lack of quantitative success must be understood in the context of all of these factors, particularly; the worldview and political factors are the most salient ones. This research is based on extended literature study and draws from multiple sources across various disciplines, sources that are in English and generally based upon the work of both Japanese and Western scholars.

Why is **Christianity** Not Widely
Believed in Japan?

The
JAPANESE
& CHRISTIANITY

Samuel **Lee**

Foundation
UNIVERSITY PRESS

The Japanese & Christianity
Why is **Christianity** Not Widely Believed in Japan

First Edition
ISBN: 978-94-90179-17-5

For permission requests, write to the publisher, addressed to
Attention: Permissions Coordinator, at the address below.

Foundation Univeristy Press
Post Office Box 12429
1100 AK Amsterdam, The Netherlands

book design | **timmyroland**.com

CONTENTS

Why is **Christianity** Not Widely
Believed in Japan?

ACKNOWLEDGMENTS

I am indebted to many people for their assistance with the writing of this thesis. My deepest gratitude is to my main supervisor, Prof. Dr. Martien Brinkman, who believed in my abilities and offered me the opportunity to conduct my Ph.D. research at the Free University Amsterdam. The hours spent in Prof. Brinkman's office discussing the chapters of my dissertation are highly memorable. They were some of the most inspiring moments of the period of my research. I always looked forward to my next meeting with him.

Furthermore, I wish to express my gratitude to Dr. J. Nelson Jennings, my co-supervisor at the Overseas Ministries Study Center in New Haven, for his supervision and guidance throughout the period of my research as well as for his friendship and kindness. I am honored to have been able to work with him.

Special thanks are due to Rev. Arimasa Kubo, at Biblical-Japan Forum, for his constructive advice communicated via email and for his friendship. My gratitude also goes to my friend and editor, Deborah S. Nash, who helped correct the flow of my English and provided critical insights and comments throughout the research process, especially relating to fields of Buddhism and interreligious dialogue. I would also like to express my appreciation to my friend Simon Pleasants for his uplifting communications and linguistic support.

Last, but not least, I wish to acknowledge my friends Don Wright of Reaching Japanese for Christ, Tim Gilman for his support in designing this book and my dear neighbors Masako-san and Pim-san for the beautiful Ikebana (the Japanese flower arrangement).

Above all, my gratitude goes to my entire family, especially my parents, whose love and support I count among the greatest joys in my life. They have always trusted in my abilities, believed in me and cared for me. I am indebted to my wife for her patience and unconditional love and for staying awake with me through the nights I was working on my dissertation, and to my two sons and my daughter for their willingness to tolerate the frequent absences from family life that were necessary to conduct this research.

PREFACE

From childhood, I have been fascinated with Japanese culture. Thus, in the 1990s as a student of Sociology of Non-Western Societies at Leiden University, I chose Japan as my regional specialization. Before I became interested in this research, I had been involved with Christian ministry for twenty years. Thus, my academic background and my passion for both Japan and Christianity have come to intersect in the book you are about to read.

Japan has been a home to Shinto, Buddhism and Confucianism for centuries. During the sixteenth, nineteenth and twentieth centuries, Christian missionaries have tried hard to share the gospel to the Japanese but did not have the desired success. The question of why, after centuries of Christian history, Christianity has not yet been successful in Japan is one that interests me greatly. As the reader will observe, it recurs regularly throughout this dissertation. Metaphorically, I compare Japan and Christianity with two lovers with a complex relationship; full of ups and downs, passion, strife, and at the same time peace, reconciliation and love.

It is my hope that, this research will contribute to a further deepening of the scholarly discussion on the overall topic of Christianity in Japan, and specifically to further clarification of the puzzle of its partial success thus far.

Amsterdam, 28 February 2014

Why is **Christianity** Not Widely
Believed in Japan?

Chapter 1

INTRODUCTION

The story of Japan and Christianity is a long and fascinating one. Since the mid-sixteenth century, Christianity has been notably active in Japan. Various statistical sources such as the *Japanese Agency for Cultural Affairs* (2011)[1] or *Operation World* (2010)[2] indicate that the percentage of Christians in Japan is between 1.40 to 1.54 percent; hence Japan is one of the least-evangelized nations in the world.

The central question of this book is, "What are the main factors why Christianity has not yet succeeded in Japan?" How could the success of Christianity be defined? Is success described in quantitative terms (e.g., statistical data), or is it expressed qualitatively (e.g., in terms of influence)? Here, I investigate various factors such as the societal, cultural, historical, missiological, and political dimensions of Christianity in Japan.[3] Some studies focus on one or more of these factors, yet they do not discuss the analytical links between them. For instance, Robert Lee searches for answers in what he calls the 'clash of civilizations' between Western Christianity and Japanese culture, especially as concerns their respective world- views and the Japanese Emperor system.[4] Mitsuo Fukuda emphasizes the contextualized church from a Japanese perspective;[5] Noriyuki Miyake reviews the Japanese social and religious life in an attempt to find answers to the problem of Christianity's lack of appeal to the Japanese.[6] Mark Mullin's project is that of comparative sociological and historical research into Christianity in modern Japanese society and indigenous Christian movements in Japan.[7]

Further, my book offers some insights into the role played by politics in the development of Christianity in Japan. Many of the objections that some Japanese people raise against Christianity relate to Western aggression, war and violence. Here I examine the connections between politics, militarism, Christianity and Japanese culture in relation to the question "why Christianity has not been widely accepted in Japan?"

1.1 Methodology

My research is based on extended literature study and draws from multiple sources across various disciplines, sources that are in English and generally based upon the work of both Japanese and Western scholars. The following authors are cited throughout this work: Mark Mullins, Ian Reader, J. Nelson Jennings, Mitsuo Fukuda, Robert Lee, Ama Toshimaro and Emi Mase-Hasegawa. I have focused on their work (along with that of many other authors) because of their high level of expertise in this field. I have also integrated the information from some relevant websites, journals, newspapers and magazines. Lastly, this book follows the Western name order, which puts the given name in front of the family name.

1.2 Definitions

1.2.1 Christianity

Throughout the book, I often use generalized terms such as "Christianity", "Western Christianity", "Christianity in Japan" or "Japanese Christianity". Most available literature on the question of Christianity and Japan uses the generic term "Christianity," even though each church prefers to use their own name.

The term "Christianity" is problematic from the start. How exactly is it defined? Can church denominations or individual Christians be said to embody Christianity? Are there particular sets of theological doctrines with which all Japanese Christians identify themselves? It is difficult to draw either a clear-cut and distinct line between the terms "Christianity", "Church" and "Christians" as well as to assert that all these terms include each other. Japanese Christianity is like Christianity everywhere — it is divided up into various denominations, each of which differs slightly with respect to tradition, doctrine, and history. It is for this reason that I have here sought to avoid strict definitions.

When I refer to Christianity, I limit myself to Roman Catholicism and Protestantism (with its variety of denominations and churches). When it comes to the doctrinal aspects of Christianity, I pay special attention to evangelicalism, because its missionary movement was strong and influential in Japan after World War II. I use the term "Western Christianity" for Roman Catholicism, Protestantism and Evangelicalism and their respective missionary endeavors throughout Japanese history.

3

Further, by "Christianity in Japan" I mean the combination of foreign missionary establishments, such as churches, mission agencies, and relief organizations, but also native churches that are "foreign-oriented." The latter includes the Anglican, Roman Catholic and Lutheran Church, the Evangelical and Pentecostal Churches and the United Church of Christ (which encompasses the Methodist, Reformed, Presbyterian, and Congregational Churches). I also include the native independent churches that are doctrinally influenced by American Evangelicalism and Pentecostalism. The Japanese Orthodox Church was deliberately omitted from consideration here since it has its own unique history. According to Mullins, "foreign-oriented" denominations still receive foreign missionaries. Their understanding of theological orthodoxy and models for church polity and organization are drawn primarily from Western churches.[8]

Lastly, by "Japanese Christianity" I mean a Christianity that has become more or less indigenized with respect to both doctrine and experience. Mullins described these Christian churches as "native-oriented." They do not measure their perception of religious truth by the standards set by Western theology or by ancient church councils.[9] Some good examples of such an indigenous version of Christianity are The Non- Church movement *(Mukyokai)*, the Way *(Dokai)*, and the Christ Heart Church *(Kirisuto Shinsho Kyodan)*.

1.2.2 The Japanese Culture

By Japanese culture, I mean the Japanese people, language, religious views, and society. It is not my intention to portray this culture as unique. Japan has its own social and cultural particularities at the same time it manifests many similarities with other cultures. Although my final conclusion will be that there is a great deal of overlap in this, for the purpose of research, I still attempt to distinguish between cultural, religious, and societal aspects of Japanese life.

1.3 Central Hypothesis

There is not one single or primary reason for Christianity's lack of success in Japan. Rather, several important factors overlap. In the following paragraphs, I outline the framework of my hypothesis by providing an introductory description of these factors.

Historical Factors (Ch. 2)

In chapter two, I provide an historical review of Christianity in Japan. I briefly present the entrance of Roman Catholicism into Japan from the late sixteenth century onward and the persecution of that faith during the Tokugawa (Edo) Period (1603–1868); I also discuss its re-entry into the country during the Meiji Period (1868–1912) and post World War II. The history of Protestantism in Japan is briefly outlined in chapter two.

Worldview Factors (Ch. 3)

In chapter three, I examine probable areas of conflict between the Japanese and Western Christian worldviews. These can be traced to extant conditions in various areas of life such as religion and culture. Corporatism is central to the Japanese worldview. Mutual benefits are sought between the group and individual and harmony is regarded as a crucial element of life. It is difficult to understand the mentality of a typical Japanese person, unless one grasps the importance of group affiliation.[10]

Three major categories of groups are vital for the individual in Japan. He or she must belong to a family and a neighborhood and have some sort of vocational affiliation such as a company, school, college or university. In Japanese culture, decisions are made based on corporatism within and between these categories. Personal decisions are not allowed to disturb the harmony of these groups even when such decisions are logically beneficial to the individual decision maker. Here, the concept of *wa* comes into play.

Further, in Japanese culture truth is often viewed as being relative. The Japanese evaluate information based on its relational context.[11] Fukuda calls this contextual logic: no religion, no view is taken to be absolute. Throughout their history, the Japanese have developed a particular way of allowing the religions of Shinto, Buddhism and Confucianism to co-exist. This is called *shinbutsuju shugo* a harmonious fusion of Buddhism, Shinto and Confucianism initiated by Prince Shotoku (574–622).[12] This concept of *shinbutsuju shugo* and religious co-existence is elaborated in chapter three.

Chapter three also discusses the concept of religion. The Japanese view of religion differs markedly from that of the West. The way they view concepts such as God, rituals, super- naturalism and life after death contradicts Christian doctrines. The Japanese people do not understand religion simply by separating it into individual components. Fukuda suggests that Shinto, Buddhism, etc. express different facets of a single, syncretized Japanese religion.[13] *Shinbutsuju shugo* also encompasses various new religions as well as the less formal traditions of Confucianism and Taoism and the beliefs of folk traditions.[14] Earhart considers this to be one "Sacred Way" that includes various traditions within it.[15]

Finally, chapter three discusses crucial differences between Japanese and Christian views of the existence of God. Fukuda suggests that, in the Christian worldview, the existence of God imparts ultimate meaning and value to everything. Nature and humanity, then, derive meaning and value from God, although they were damaged by the sin of man at the beginning of creation. In contrast, the Japanese worldview insists that human life and nature are valuable in and of themselves, and views sin as a partial, contemporary stain on the surface of the person. Human life is an entity in and of itself and is valued apart from any relationship with a transcendent God.[16]

Theological Factors (Ch. 4)

In chapter four, I examine fundamental theological concepts such as sin, life after death, ancestor veneration, and the claims of the exclusiveness of Christ and discuss these in context of Japanese culture and religion. Some of these concepts are in direct conflict with Japanese religious views.

Sin, for instance, is considered to be a disturbance of the harmony between gods and a given group of people. The word that the Japanese use for "sin" is *tsumi*, which is the same word used for "crime". So, when an evangelist or a missionary claims, "we all have sinned" or "we are all sinners," the average Japanese may actually not understand what is being said — he or she does not consider himself a "criminal". I believe that the concept of sin is more or less unique to the Abrahamic faiths with their origins in the Middle East. Sin is considered to be disobedience of God's laws. Yet, how can sin be understood if the concept of God differs from that in Judeo–Christian traditions, and if it is presented without the concept of "law", which is also connected to the Judeo–Christian God? In chapter four, I therefore discuss further the concept of sin in Japanese culture.

Another problem that is discussed in chapter four is the question of what happened to the Japanese people who died before they had the chance to hear the gospel? Almost every Japanese who is evangelized by Western missionaries asks this question. Of course, missionaries try to answer it as sensitively as possible, but ultimately they have to mention the word "hell". A Japanese woman once told a missionary who was trying to evangelize her that she would rather spend eternity in hell with her ancestors than in the paradise preached by Christians. If the Christian God has no solution to the fact that her ancestors did not have a chance to hear about Jesus, she would rather spend all eternity in hell. In the Japanese worldview, ancestors are to be venerated; in Christian doc- trine, salvation is by choice. Hence, if this choice disturbs the harmony with the family's ancestors, then it is then hard for a Japanese to openly become a Christian.

There have been many attempts to address this theological doctrine from the perspective of Japanese culture. One of the most recent ones is the so-called *Sekundo Chansu Ron* or Second Chance Theory. The Second Chance Theory proposes salvation for the dead, especially those who have never had a chance to hear the gospel (in Japan's case, the ancestors). I discuss the Second Chance Theory in Chapter four.

Missiological Factors (Ch. 5)

Chapter five focuses on missiological factors. It describes the manner in which Christianity has been introduced to the Japanese people throughout their history. The answer to the question of why Christianity has not yet succeeded in Japan can be found partly in the way the Christian mission has been conducted in Japan throughout history.

Western Christianity, in all its forms and varieties, has played a dominant role in transmitting the Christian message by sending out missionaries around the globe. Robert Lee suggests that enlightenment in the West envisioned the world as a homogeneous entity, a vision that was reinforced by the rise of the world market in the nineteenth century after the coming of the industrial revolution.[17]

In relation to this dominance, I identify the following major errors committed by Western missionaries in Japan in the past: (1) a Eurocentric approach; (2) a lack of consideration for cultural context; and (3) denominational competitiveness. These will be discussed in chapter five.

Societal Factors (Ch. 6)

In chapter six, I review social factors such as family obligations and neighborhood duties as well as occupational and educational participation of most Japanese people in relation to Christianity.

9

There are several factors why organized Christianity has not succeeded in Japan. In chapter six, I discuss what I consider to be the three most important ones: Japanese family life, working life, and education.

Nuclear families living in large cities also engage in various activities, such as school activities for children and neighborhood activities, which are crucial for ensuring group harmony and avoiding shame and disgrace to the family. For this reason, the average Japanese family may not have enough time to participate in additional Christian activities such as church services, mid-week prayer meetings, and other events. The requirement of attending church on a weekly basis may be quite burdensome. This alone discourages people from accepting and practicing Christianity.

The Japanese are known as an industrious people. They work long hours and are almost never absent from their jobs. This is the image many have of their workforce. A Japanese employee is generally referred to as a *salaryman*, an English loan word. In chapter six, I explain why becoming a Christian and practicing Christianity may not be an easy option for a Japanese, especially for someone from the working class.

The Japanese educational system has generated a great deal of debate among scholars and educators. Some praise it, while others criticize it. Some believe that the strong emphasis it places on the group and on unity results in the individuality of each child being ignored. In chapter six, I describe Japan's education system and discuss the effect it may have on Christianization efforts.

Political Factors (Ch. 7)

In chapter seven, I discuss the possible role played by political factors in the reception of Christianity by Japan, both in the past and present. Throughout history, most Japanese have viewed it as the religion of the West. Since World War II, Christianity has been associated with America in particular — the nation that utilized two nuclear bombs on civilians to end the war. Thus, it is viewed as the religion of the occupying "messiah", a nation that has deliberately forgotten its dark past, (the eradication of the native peoples in the Americas, slavery, racism and segregation), and yet accuses Japan of genocide, war crimes and acts of cruelty in the course of human history.

In Japan, Christianity and the West are conflated and considered to be inseparable. For most Japanese people, Christianity remains a Western religion that is used by Western political powers to expand their influence and gain control of other nations.

Christianity's Contribution to Japan (Ch. 8)

In chapter eight, I describe some of the positive contributions Christianity has made to Japanese culture and society. I dis- cuss four major areas of influence: education, social justice, theology, and intellectual life. I describe the position that native Christian artists, human rights activists, and even some prime ministers have acquired in the Japanese culture and society. In doing this, I hope to present a more balanced view of Christianity in Japan by considering not only the conflicting factors in its reception, but also the positive influence it has had on that culture.

11

Final Reflections (Ch. 9)

Based on what has been presented in previous chapters, chapter nine offers final remarks and conclusions concerning Christianity's lack of quantitative success in Japan. In purely numerical terms, Christianity has not been successful in Japan. This is simply a reality. However, in the end, success understood in purely quantitative terms may not count for more than influence-oriented success.

Finally, this book intends to add some new insight to the existing body of knowledge on the question of why, after almost five centuries, Christianity is still not widely accepted and practiced in Japan. The research upon which it rests allows one to make sense of the various cultural, political and religious factors which are at play in the Japanese situation. It corroborates and elaborates upon them, then draws them together and shows that their combination contributes to a better understanding the complex relationship between Japan and Christianity.

Notes

1 Japanese Agency for Cultural Affairs, (2011). Religious Juridical Persons and Administration of Religious Affairs. http://www.bunka. go.jp/english/pdf/h24_chapter_11.pdf accessed 27 August 2013.

2 Jason Mandryk, *Operation World: The Definitive Prayer Guide to Every Nation,* 7th edition (Colorado Springs: Biblica Publishing, 2010), 489. For my research, I prefer Operation World report 2010, because it gives more extended information about the overall condition of Christianity in Japan.

3 Additional items might have been suitable for discussion here, but these seemed to most relevant and most in need of elaboration.

4 Robert Lee, *The Clash of Civilizations: An Intrusive Gospel in Japanese Civilization* (Harrisburg: Trinity Press International, 1999).

5 Mitsuo Fukuda, *Developing A Contextualized Church As A Bridge to Christianity in Japan* (Gloucester: Wide Margin, 2012).

6 Noriyuki Miyake, *Belong, Experience, Believe: Pentecostal Mission Strategies for Japan* (Gloucester: Wide Margin, 2005).

7 Mark R. Mullins, *Christianity Made in Japan: A Study of Indigenous Movements* (H-ligion at the Faculty of Arts – School of Asian Studies at the University of Auckland, New Zealand and has written numerous books and articles. *Christianity Made in Japan* (1998) is one of his most well-known studies.

8 Mark R. Mullins, "Christianity as a New Religion: Charisma, Minor Founders, and Indigenous Movements" in *Religion and Society in Modern Japan*, eds. Mark R. Mullins, Shimazono Susumu, Paul L. Swanson (Eds.) (Fremont: Asian Humanities Press, 1993), 257–72.

9 Ibid.

10 Noriyuki Miyake, *Belong, Experience, Believe: Pentecostal Mission Strategies for Japan* (Gloucester: Wide Margin, 2005), 12.

11 Mitsuo Fukuda, *Developing A Contextualized Church As A Bridge to Christianity in Japan* (Gloucester: Wide Margin, 2012), 52.

12 Ibid.

13 Fukuda, 45.

14 Fukuda, 44.

15 H.B. Earhart, *Religions of Japan: Many Traditions Within One Sacred Way* (New York: Harper and Row, 1984).

16 Fukuda, 45.

17 Robert Lee, *The Clash of Civilizations: An Intrusive Gospel in Japanese Civilization* (Harrisburg: Trinity Press International, 1999), 102.

Chapter 2

A BRIEF HISTORICAL REVIEW

At this point, I briefly discuss the history of Christianity in Japan. This will facilitate reading of the following chapters by giving an historical perspective, as they contain frequent references to periods in Japanese history.

2.1 The Tokugawa Period (1603–1868)

It was at the end of sixteenth century that Japan encountered the West for the first time.[1] By the end of the sixteenth century, Japan was a decentralized nation ruled by military overlords and peasant confederations. Ieyasu Tokugawa, put an end to this decentralized Japan. His victory at the Battle of Sekigahara in 1600 marks the start of the Tokugawa Period, which lasted for more than 250 years.[2] He and his descendants were able to place Japan under the centralized leadership of the *Shogun*. During these 250 years, Japanese society was classified into various strata and everyone was required to belong to a certain social class. This stratification was based on Confucian ethics combined with Buddhist principles. These provided the moral standards for daily living and religious beliefs in Japan.[3]

2.1.1 The Arrival of Roman Catholicism

The history of Roman Catholic Japan in the Tokugawa Period is generally divided into two major episodes: "The Christian Century"

15

(1549–1639) and "The Underground Period" or *Senpuku Jidai* (1640–1837). After Portuguese seafarers landed in Japan by chance in 1542, the Jesuits quickly set their sights on this new land. Members of the newly formed Jesuit Society were known for their strict discipline, unconditional loyalty to the Pope, and fearless promotion of their version of Christian faith.

In 1548, Anjiro, a 36-year-old man, fled Japan after committing murder. He boarded a Portuguese ship bound for India. There he met Francis Xavier, a Portuguese priest, who had been sent by the King of Portugal as a missionary to the Europeans and Indians in Malacca, a Portuguese territory.[4] Aboard the boat, Xavier asked Anjiro: "If I went to Japan, would the people become Christians?" Anjiro replied:

> My people would not immediately become Christians, but they would first ask you a multitude of questions, weighing carefully your answers and your claims. Above all, they would observe whether your conduct agrees with your words. If you could satisfy them on these points by suitable replies to their inquiries and by a life above reproach, then, as soon as the matter was known and fully examined, the warlord (*daimyo*), the nobles, and the educated people would become Christians. Six months would suffice; for the nation is one that always follows the guidance of reason.[5]

Upon his arrival in 1549, Francis Xavier was given a friendly reception by one of the powerful lords of the land—Shimazu Takahisa—at

Ijuin and was allowed to preach Christianity and convert people. The priest's sterling character was pivotal to his success.[6] The lords and their ministers as well as influential monks were charmed by Xavier's charisma and strength. Political factors worked in his favor as well. Merchants and cargo ships followed the Jesuits into Japan, and the shoguns—warlords—made certain they profited from such commerce.

During his two years in the country, Xavier saw the conversion of 1,000 Japanese and laid the foundation for the missionary work of the Jesuits who later replaced him.[7] Eager to proselytize in China, he left Japan in 1551. He later wrote that, in many respects, the Japanese were superior to Europeans and referred to them as "the delight of my heart."[8] Nothing can describe the beginnings of the Jesuit missions in Japan as vividly as the letters of Xavier himself. On November 5, 1549, ten weeks after having arrived there, he wrote:

> "By the experience which we have had of this land of Japan, I can inform you thereof as follows—firstly the people whom we have met so far, are the best who have as yet been discovered, and it seems to me we shall never find among heathens another race to equal the Japanese. They are people of very good manners, good in general, and not malicious; they are men of honor to a marvel, and prize honor above all else in the world. They have one quality which I cannot recall in any people of Christendom;

this is that their gentry howsoever poor they be, and commoners howsoever rich they be, render as much as honor to a poor gentleman as if he were passing rich. Whence it can clearly be seen that they esteem honor more than riches."[9]

In Xavier's opinion, the beginning of the Jesuit mission was relatively successful, despite the cultural and linguistic problems it encountered. He also suggests that the Japanese themselves had been questioning the various sects that existed in their country, and that the Jesuits arrived with yet one more alternative, namely Roman Catholicism.[10]

Initially, Xavier and his companions communicated the most basic elements of the Judeo–Christian faith such as creation and the law. Xavier's letter also indicates that Japanese interest in Christianity began among some wealthy and mighty warlords, a fact which facilitated the involvement of Roman Catholicism in politics and the economy in certain regions of the country. For example, some Kyushu daimyo, like the daimyo of Omura, favored the missionaries in an effort to attract trade to their domains. They embraced Christianity and forced the people in their domains to also become Christians.[11]

The daimyo of Omura who was converted to Christianity in 1562, founded the port of Nagasaki and made it the center of Portuguese trade.[12] In 1579 he assigned the control of the town to the Jesuits.[13] This may have been advantageous to the Jesuits, but, at the same time, it produced enmity toward Roman Catholic

Christianity—on the part of the established Japanese religious leadership as well as some warlords who opposed those who accepted Christianity or sympathized with it.[14]

In 1553, there were five missionaries in the country and the number of converts in three separate regions was approximately 4,000. By 1579, they numbered 100,000, even though there were only fifty-five missionaries in all of Japan at that time.[15] In 1614, before the period of persecution started in earnest, there may have been as many as 370,000 Catholic Christians in the country (nearly two percent of the population); they were largely concentrated in Kyushu. Some converts were educated men and some were politically powerful, particularly the Christian daimyo and the warlords such as Takayama Ukon, but most were peasants who became Christians at the behest of their warlords.[16]

One of the successors of Xavier was a certain Portuguese Jesuit named Father Valignano; his first visit to Japan was between 1579 and 1582. He approached the Japanese by avoiding cultural friction and compromising with those of their customs that conflicted with Catholic values. His strategy was to prevent representatives of the mendicant orders (e.g., the Franciscans and Dominicans) from entering the country.[17] The Jesuits had enjoyed exclusive dominion over missionary activities there for 30 years; the papal brief *Ex Pastoralis Officio* of 1585, issued by Pope Gregory XIII, had guaranteed them this exclusivity.[18] Nevertheless, other missionaries soon joined the Jesuits: the first Franciscan mission was established in 1593[19], and the Dominicans and Augustinians followed later. The arrival of the three groups of friars marked the beginning of bitter rivalry and territorialism. It was particularly fierce between the Jesuits and the Franciscans.[20] The Franciscans, Dominicans, and Augustinians were well informed of the successes of the Jesuits in Japan and were desperately anxious to harvest from that field —partly out of jealousy and partly out of the conviction that they could repair the political damage that had been done by the Jesuits. In fact, they considered the Jesuits' errors to be the true cause of Hideyoshi's persecution in 1587.[21]

In 1591, Hideyoshi, one of the historic figures who unified the nation of Japan, sent an envoy to the governor of Manila, Gomez Perez de Marinas. He was carrying a letter that warned the Philippines to prepare for war. It informed the governor that, after Hideyoshi conquered Korea and China, he would turn on the Philippines. In response, the governor of Manila sent a small mission to Japan headed by Franciscan Father Juan Cobos. This did not satisfy Hideyoshi at all.[22] In 1593, the governor of Manila sent another envoy, headed by Franciscan Father Pedro Batista together with three other Franciscans. The letter they carried was taken more seriously this time since it expressed a desire on the part of the King of Spain to open trade with Japan.[23]

According to Sansom, the four Franciscans thereupon offered to remain in Japan as hostages and asked for permission to reside and preach in the home provinces. This was granted and they soon established a church in Kyoto and a convent in Osaka. Joined by two more Franciscans, they then tried to establish themselves in Nagasaki, but without success. At that time, Hideyoshi issued a ban on Jesuits; they would be tolerated only in Nagasaki solely for the spiritual needs of the Portuguese.[24] The Franciscans did not respect this ban and preached throughout the land, thus breaking the law at every turn. Hideyoshi took no steps against them, a fact which fueled the anger of the Jesuits against the Franciscans. The anger of Hideyoshi, was however, aroused by the brutal language of the captain of a wrecked ship. He complained about the treatment of the vessel and its extremely valuable cargo, which had fallen into the hands of the lord of Tosa and Hideyoshi, himself. The captain left for Osaka to seek remedy from Hideyoshi, but used reckless language in addressing him. He threatened Hideyoshi and boasted that the long arm of the law (i.e., the King of Spain) would soon arrive in Japan and Japanese Christians would rise up in his favor. He also added that the missionaries were there to prepare Japan for conquest.[25]

In 1598, twenty-two Dutch vessels departed for the Far East. Due to a storm, one of them ended up in Bungo, Japan. The name of that ship was De Liefde, meaning Love or Charity; it was captained by Jacob Quaeckernaeck and piloted by Englishman, Will Adams. Upon its unexpected arrival there, the Portuguese Jesuits immediately traveled to the port city from Nagasaki to act as interpreters.[26] Of course, one can imagine that this was hardly advantageous to the Dutch given the troubled history between the Netherlands and Spain. However, contrary to the expectations of the Jesuits, the *daimyo* treated them kindly.[27] The Dutch were primarily interested in trade and did not have a religious agenda. This was less threatening to the Japanese. In the course of the few centuries of their interaction with Japan, the Dutch gradually made Western science and technology available to the Japanese.

21

2.1.2 Toward the Era of Persecution

The missionaries were not always tolerant toward the culture of their host nation, a fact which stirred up opposition from the Buddhist clergy. This also led to sporadic persecution of Christians by the political authorities. Nevertheless, the religion spread rapidly throughout Japan, most markedly in Kyushu and the Kyoto area. The Japanese were conscious of having learned much from abroad—that is, from China—and so they were also open to Western ideas; goods other than those produced in Asian societies were also welcomed. Indeed, the country became the Jesuits' most promising missionary field in Asia.[28]

Eventually, the bond between the Japanese Christians and the Pope caused the Japanese leaders to view Christianity as a potentially subversive force[29] and so they started to persecute Christians and systematically attempt to eliminate them from the country. This hostility did not, however, develop overnight; rather, it was part of an historic process. Various factors contributed to this decision on the part of the Japanese authorities—one which resulted in almost 250 years of persecution. The persecution of Christians toward the end of the sixteenth century and the Tokugawa Period—an era when Christians went into hiding—is discussed in chapter five. These hidden Christians *(kakure Kirishitan[30])* clearly possessed the hallmarks of the Japanese character.

The tensions that developed on the international scene at this time made the rulers of unified Japan suspicious of the intentions of any European residing in their country. Seeing what the Spanish and the Portuguese had done in other countries, and noting the obvious parallels between colonization and evangelization, the Japanese authorities were not pleased. They were not comfortable with the Christians who would likely remain loyal to an external religious figure—the Pope—as their leader while, at the same time, swearing loyalty to the Spanish king. In their view, this could amount to a sort of fifth column, a Trojan horse, and might eventually lead to the overthrow of Japan.[31] Hence, the Tokugawa regime deliberately eliminated Christianity and basically closed the nation's doors to Europeans. The Dutch constituted the only exception to this ban. Since they did not have a religious agenda and were already under heavy restrictions regarding their interaction with the Japanese— they were restricted to engaging in the activity of trade only.

Missionaries were deported, some were killed, and many newly converted Christians remained spiritually fatherless, without guidance from experts. On January 27, 1614, Ieyasu Tokugawa's son, Hidetada, issued a further edict banning Christianity altogether. It demanded the immediate deportation of all foreign missionaries, and commanded the local *daimyo* to destroy Christian churches; also, Japanese Christians were forced to return to their national religions.[32]Persecution of Christians in Japan had been conducted in the form of organized terror and systematic executions.

Gradually, Christians went underground, producing one of the most fascinating phenomena in Christian history: *kakure Kirishitans* (i.e., "hidden Christians"). In various parts of Japan, there were Christian communities and even villages that maintained their Christian faith for almost 250 years. Some remained undiscovered by the authorities until the Meiji Period. Throughout the years, they developed their own ways of life, ceremonies, and religious practices. *Kakure Kirishitans* have long fascinated scholars and historians, both inside and outside of Japan.

2.2 Meiji Period (1868–1912)

The Meiji Period began with an ambitious program aiming to transform Japan into a modern, centralized nation state in keeping with the West-European model—it would be a strong military and economic power, even competing with European states.[33] The Meiji Period was characterized by the slogans *bunmei kaika* (which means civilization and enlightenment), *fukoku kyohei* (a rich nation with a strong army), and *oitsuki oikose* (catch up and pass; i.e., catch up with and surpass the West). Intellectual groups arose that viewed the West as offering civilization, science, and technology. [34]

One of the leading intellectuals of this period was Yukichi Fukuzawa (1835-1901).[35] He wrote several books on Western culture, two of his important works being "An Outline of Civilization," and "Encouragement of Learning". Fukuzawa visited Western countries and described his observations of buildings, institutions, factories, streets, technology, etc. in his books. Such things captured the imagination of the Japanese people. He believed that education was the foundation of modernity. He also founded one of the prestigious universities of Japan — Keio University. However, while people like Fukuzawa accepted Western civilization, they also strongly believed in maintaining Japanese culture and religion.

Others had different opinions. Christianity attracted many inquiring Japanese intellectuals from the samurai class, such as

Joseph Niishima (1843-1890) or Inazo Nitobe (1862-1933), who saw in Christianity the key to Western progress. They believed that Protestant Christianity offered a new code of personal ethics and loyalty that would strengthen Japan.[36] They believed that the Western model without Christianity and its values was empty and that Japan's modernization should progress in conjunction with accepting and adopting the Christian faith in Japan. However, others did not accept his ideas. They believed in a combination of "Eastern ethics" and "Western science".[37] For example in 1889 Katsunan Kuga (1856-1907), writes in the newspaper *Nihon* (Japan):

> We recognize the excellence of the Western civilization. We value the Western theories of rights, liberty and equality; and we respect Western philosophy and morals . . . Above all, we esteem Western science, economy and industry. These however, ought not to be adopted simply because they are Western; they ought to be adopted only if they can contribute to Japan's welfare.[38]

Soon a group of intellectuals formed for the purpose of initiating reform in Japan. The central figures in the newly formed government came from various circles in society and they campaigned forcefully for the restoration of the Emperor's legitimate power and influence in national politics. These men were influenced by the writings and teachings of Fukuzawa and other scholars.

Japan began to change drastically. The legal system changed.

People were considered equal according to the new law and the old classes were no longer significant. However, this did not mean that Japanese people had totally abandoned their 250 years old class system. It was impossible to change to the new system immediately. However, the political atmosphere changed in the 1870s when the first political parties were formed.

2.2.1 The Arrival of Protestantism

It was during Meiji Period that Protestantism entered Japan. Commodore Perry from America opened the doors for the various Protestant churches to become established in Japan. Their missionaries first arrived during the final years of the Tokugawa Period. As mentioned earlier, at that point, Japan had been isolated from the rest of the world (with the exception of some Dutch) for approximately 250 years. This was therefore an opportunity for the West to once again engage with the country.

Perry was sent to Japan by the American government for several factors. First, he was to ensure that the country could be used as a "coaling base", a point from which coal-consuming steamships could refill their supplies en route to and from China. Japan's geographical location was perfect for this purpose.[39] Second, trade was a crucial concern. It produced a great deal of revenue for the Americans and they wanted to expand their trading networks. Perry was indeed successful in persuading the Japanese to open up their gates to foreigners, especially Americans. Third, the Americans wanted to establish ties with Japan in order to make sure the sailors who suffered shipwreck in Japan received good treatment.[40]

A whaling ship called the Lagoda had been shipwrecked there many years earlier and many of its sailors had been treated badly.

Perry's success with the Japanese aroused great enthusiasm among Christians in America, and the question of sending missionaries to this newly opened country was seriously discussed among the churches and mission organizations.[41] This enthusiasm was, however, short lived. It soon turned into temporary disappointment when it was learned that Perry's treaty had not secured the right of permanent residence or religious freedom for Americans in Japan. As long as these were not in place, Christian missionaries could not establish stations in Japan. Of course, the Japanese did not have a good impression of Christianity as it had been brought to them by other Western nations during the sixteenth century.[42]

Pressure from the American and other Western governments eventually caused the Japanese government to grant the missionaries permission to re-establish themselves there again. For a relatively short period of time, they were allowed to evangelize and create churches within very limited port areas. Protestant missionary work was initiated in 1858 by the American Presbyterian and Reformed churches. During 1880s and 1890s, more missionaries arrived from Europe and North America. At the 1890 synod, the Church of Christ in Japan *(Nihon Kirisuto Kyokai)* became a reality.[43]

2.3 Taisho Period (1912–1926) & Early Showa Period (1926–1945)

During the Taisho Period (1912–1926), Japan shifted from an

oligarchical political system to a parliamentary one with a diet and political parties. This period in Japanese history is also known as the Taisho Democracy. Thus, "the relatively free atmosphere of the Taisho years contributed to steady church growth, particularly among the increasing white-collar, educated city dwellers."[44] Such growth was further facilitated by cooperative evangelistic efforts. The Taisho Period was also a period of interdenominational evangelistic work. In 1922, for instance the ecumenical movement in Japan formed the National Christian Council (NCC). It included most Protestant denominations, Christian schools and social institutions.[45]NCC played a crucial role in coordinating the cooperative activities of the Protestant movement.[46] It also played a role in conducting relief operations for Christian churches after the 1923 Great Kanto Earthquake. Internationally, NCC also presented reasoned Christian protests against the United States Congress's 1924 Anti-Immigration Bill. Further, it was deeply involved in supporting evangelistic initiatives.[47]

The Showa Period (1926–1989) corresponds with the period of the reign of the Showa Emperor, Hirohito from (December 1926– end January 1989). This era is divided into pre- and post-World War II periods, the latter beginning after Japan's surrender in 1945.

From the early years of the Showa Period (the late 1930s), the Japanese government became increasingly totalitarian. During this period, State Shinto was established as a "National Religion". This differed considerably from the previous forms of Shinto belief and practice.[48] It was used, nevertheless, to unify and integrate the heterogeneous population and mobilize the people for nation

building, modernization, and military expansion.[49] According to the
Religious Organization Law that was promulgated during the early
Showa Period, the members of religious organizations were obliged
to participate in civil religious rituals and conform to State Shinto.
Mullins Writes:

> Given the legal measures and intense government
> pressures noted above, it is not surprising that most
> transplanted churches and Christian institutions
> gradually accommodated themselves to the
> nationalistic environment. After varying degrees of
> resistance to the claims of the state, the Roman
> Catholic Church and most Protestant denominations
> eventually instructed their members to participate in
> the rituals of civil religion. By the late 1930s most
> churches had also created some form of theological
> rhetoric to legitimize the Imperial Way, including
> support for Japanese military expansionism.[50]

Thus, with the implementation of the Religious Organization Law, all
Protestant churches were united under *Nippon Kirisuto Kyodan*, later
referred to as *Kyodan* or the United Church. This so-called unity was
achieved in 1941 by force of law.

At the end of World War II, these religious laws were
abolished, and the Episcopal, Lutheran and parts of the Baptist
and Holiness churches, together with the Salvation Army, were
allowed to separate from the United Church. Some of the holiness

groups remained separate indefinitely. The majority of the leaders of the *Nihon Kirisuto Kyokai* wanted the United Church to become a federal union, but this proposal was rejected. In 1951, thirty-nine congregations excluded themselves from the United Church and re-established the *Nihon Kirisuto Kyokai*.[51]

2.4 Post-World War II Japan

With the end of the Pacific War and the start of the Occupation of Japan by the Allied Forces in 1945, missionaries resumed their activities. The post-war constitution guaranteed freedom of religion and separation of church and state. Christians in Japan did not have it easy reintroducing Christianity during the rebuilding process. However, substantial co-operation between missionaries and church leaders fostered the recovery of the Japanese church. At the same time, their combined relief work encouraged many non-Christian Japanese to see Christianity in a positive light, as a pacifist, liberal influence in the nation.[52] According to Sherrill, as the church sought to address the physical needs of the people, many Japanese discovered spiritual fulfillment in Christian community.

The early post-war years are often recognized as a Christian "boom" period. Michael Sherrill indicates that, by 1948, the membership in the Roman Catholic Church of Japan was back to its 1941 figure of about 121,000 (despite the fact that 10,000 members of this community had been victims of the war); by 1951, it had grown to 157,241. During the same time period, the Protestant church established 156 new churches; in 1951, it reported 15,765 baptisms in 1,480 churches. Membership continued to grow through the 1950s and 1960s, but at a substantially slower rate.[53] On the other hand, missionaries that came to Japan formed independent mission agencies, such as Navigators or The Evangelical Missionary Alliance (TEAM) held conservative views concerning evangelism in Japan.[54]

After World War II, it remained the case that the vast majority of the Japanese did not choose Christianity as their religion. The physical as well as spiritual damage done to the population and culture as a result of the war was immense and could not be healed in just a short time. The atomic bomb dropped on Nagasaki devastated the oldest center of Christianity in the country. This, of course, further complicated the Japanese views of Christianity: how could the West, which "represented" Christianity in the eyes of the Japanese, destroy a city that had such a rich history of Christian culture and a large Christian population? This point will be discussed at greater length in chapter seven.

Since the end of the 1960s, Japan's United Church of Christ, *Kyodan*, has become ever more involved in religious political affairs of the country. In 1967, Kyodan issued an official apology for its support of aggression during war.[55] In 1969, in an official statement it expressed its concerns about the Yasukuni Bill, indicating that such a bill was a stimulus to the revival of the pre-war State Shinto. Also, the Roman Catholic Church along with Protestant community collaborated in joint campaigns against the re-nationalization of the Yasukuni Shine[56], against censorship of textbooks that minimized the appearance of Japanese war responsibilities, and against the requirement that the *Kimigayo* (the "unofficial" national anthem with imperialistic overtones) being sung at public school ceremonies.[57]

During the 1980s, *Kyodan* strengthened its relationship with Korean churches in Japan and in Korea. Also, the links between *Kyodan* and other Asian churches like in Taiwan and the Philippines were intensified. Its aim was to stimulate the spirit of reconciliation between Japan and the nations that had suffered under its military aggression.[58]

In 1990s and early 2000s, the Christian population was rapidly aging and the churches tried to survive this crisis. Thus, they focused more on evangelism by highlighting societal concerns. Since the tsunami of March 2011, the Christian churches and missionary agencies have been centered on relief work combined with evangelistic efforts. Through this devastating tsunami and the related nuclear calamities, the Christian church once again saw the need for humanitarian work.

Today, Japan's Christian community consists of Catholics, Protestants, Independents, Anglicans, Orthodox, Evangelicals, Charismatics, Pentecostals, and members of indigenous Christian denominations. Depending on one's working definition of "Christian," and despite all the evangelistic efforts that have been made throughout the years, the percentage of the Christian population in Japan still fluctuates between 1.40[59] and 1.54.[60]

Notes

1 Sir George B. Sansom, *Japan: A Short Cultural History* (Stanford: Stanford University Press, 1978), 416.

2 Edwin O. Reischauer and Albert M. Craig, *Japan: Tradition &*

Transformation (St. Leonards: Allen & Unwin Pty Ltd., 1989), 80.
Centralization of Japan was a gradual process. Three successive
military leaders; Oda Nobunaga (1534-1582), Hideyoshi (1536-1598),
and Tokugawa Ieyasu (1542-1616), building on each other's work,
unified Japan.

3 Sansom, 81.

4 Carolyn Bowen Francis and John Masaaki Nakajima, *Christians in
Japan* (New York: Friendship Press Inc., 1991), 8.

5 Ibid.

6 C.R. Boxer, *The Christian Century in Japan 1549–1650*, (Manchester:
Carcanet Press Limited, 1993), 39.

7 Ibid.

8 Ibid.

9 Henry James Coleridge, ed., *The Life and Letters of St. Francis Xavier,*
2nd Ed. Vol.2. (London: Burns & Oats, 1890).

10   Ibid.

11   Reischauer and Craig, 75.

12   Ibid.

13   Ibid.

14   Boxer 1993, 37-39.

15   Christal Whelan, trans., *Tenchi Hajimari no Koto: Beginning
of Heaven and Earth; the Sacred Book of Japan's Hidden Christians*
(Honolulu: University of Hawaii Press, 1996), 6.

16   Bowring and Kornicki, 39.

17   Boxer, 159.

18   Boxer, 160.

19   Boxer. 161.

20   Whelan, 6.

21   Sansom, 372.

22   Sansom, 373.

23   Ibid.

24   Sansom, 350.

25   Sansom, 374.

26   Boxer, 285.

27   Boxer, 289.

28   Reischauer and Craig, 75.

29   Ibid.

30   After the Shimabara Rebellion in the 1630s, Catholic Christianity
was strictly prohibited. Japanese Christians were systematically
persecuted and martyred. The harsh rules of the Tokugawa regime
forced Japanese Christians to live undercover for almost 250 years.
They therefore developed clandestine means of worship and
expressing their faith and participating in religious rites.

34

Eventually, because of the lack of missionaries and biblical literature, Christian biblical stories were transformed into Japanese versions and interpretations thereof. These were then passed from generation to generation—and this continues even today. These Christians are called the *kakure Kirishitan* or the hidden Christians. They developed their own liturgy, ceremonies, and rites.

31   Boxer, 151.

32   Ann M. Harrington, *Japan's Hidden Christians* (Chicago: Loyola University Press, 1993), 26.

33   Reischauer and Craig, 145.

34   Reischauer and Craig, 136.

35   Reischauer and Craig,162.

36   Reischauer and Craig, 159.

37   Reischauer and Craig, 160.

38   W.G. Beasley, *The Rise of Modern Japan* (London: Weidenfeld and Nicolson, 1990), 99. Beasley refers to translation of the quote in Kenneth B. Pyle, *The New Generation in Meiji Japan* (1885-1895) (Stanford: Stanford University Press), 94.

39   Richard Storry, *A History of Modern Japan* (London: Penguin Books, 1990), 85.

40   Ibid.

41   Helen J. Ballhatchet, "The Modern Missionary Movement in Japan: Roman Catholic, Protestant, Orthodox," in *Handbook of Christianity i in Japan,* ed. Mark R. Mullins (Boston: Brill, 2003), 35.

42 Ballhatchet, 36.

43 Ballhatchet, 49.

44 Hisakazu Inagaki and J. Nelson Jennings, *Philosophical Theology and East-West Dialogue* (Amsterdam: Editions Rodopi B.V.), 14.

45 A. Hamish Ion, "The Cross under an Imperial Sun Imperialism, Nationalism, and Japanese Christianity, 1895–1945," in *Handbook of Christianity in Japan*, ed. Mark R. Mullins (Boston: Brill, 2003), 75.

46 Ibid.

47 Ibid.

48 Mark R. Mullins, *Christianity Made in Japan: A Study of Indigenous Movements* (Honolulu: University of Hawaii, 1998), 19.

49 Ibid.

50 Mullins, 20.

51 "World Council of Churches" last visited 11 September, 2013. http://www.oikoumene.org/en/member-churches/united-church-of-christ-in-japan

52 Michael John Sherrill, "Christian Churches in Post-War Japan" in *Handbook of Christianity in Japan* Mark Mullins (Ed.) (Leiden: Brill Academic Publishers, 2003), 164.

53 Sherrill, 165.

54 Sherrill, 166.

55   Sherrill, 167.

56   Yasukuni Shrine is a shrine to war dead (both civilians in service and government officials) who served Japan's Emperor during wars from 1867–1951. Both the officials and citizens of the neighboring countries like Korea and China react negatively, every time a Japanese high rank official visits the Yasukuni Shrine. Thus, Yasukuni is at the center of an international controversy.

57   Sherrill, 173.

58   Sherrill, 172.

59   Japanese Agency for Cultural Affairs, (2011). Religious Juridical Persons and Administration of Religious Affairs. http://www.bunka. go.jp/english/pdf/h24_chapter_11.pdf accessed 27 August 2013.

60   Mandryk, 489.

Why is **Christianity** Not Widely
Believed in Japan?

Chapter 3

FACTORS IN THE JAPANESE WORLDVIEW

A worldview is a set of general assumptions from which a person sees and interprets the world; it is also a collection of beliefs about life and the universe as held by an individual or a group, or by citizens of a certain region or country. These ideas include natural philosophy; fundamental, existential, and normative postulates; or themes, values, emotions, and ethics.[1]

Worldview is not merely a collocation of separate, independent, unrelated believes, but is instead an intertwined, interrelated, interconnected system of beliefs.[2] Worldviews may differ in nuance and form, even within a specific geographical region, but they are also shared by all members of a certain group or across geographical regions. Thus, one can speak of the Japanese worldview within the larger context of the Asian worldview, or the Dutch worldview within a Western context. Further, it is worthwhile to mention that religion is part of a worldview; it does not constitute a worldview.

By the Japanese worldview, I mean a generalization of worldviews within Japanese culture and tradition. Even though we cannot speak of absolute worldviews, I have chosen to generalize on this to some degree in order to compare these respective worldviews. I do this by identifying areas of conflict and determining what role these conflicts play in Japanese Christianity.

This chapter discusses only two aspects of the Japanese worldview: culture and religion. In and of themselves, these play an important role in the social behavior of the Japanese people; however, they also give us a clearer understanding of why Christianity has not yet succeeded in Japan. Here I limit myself to discussing only those aspects of Japanese culture and religion that are pertinent for this research.

3.1 Cultural Aspects of the Japanese Worldview

3.1.1 Corporatism and Wa

In chapter one, I briefly stated, that corporatism is one of the factors in Japanese worldview that works against the acceptance of Christianity. *Wa* recognizes that people are not one, yet it expresses the desire for unity by practicing and respecting harmony. *Wa* is harmony or domestic peace, which starts from the needs of the social whole rather than the autonomous individual.[3]

According to Harold Perkin, "*Wa* does not seek to embody itself in individual rights or concrete rational law. From the individual's point of view it is an emotional attachment to the group—the family, community, working team, firm, nation—and an expectation that effort, cooperation, and loyalty will be rewarded by the group's permanent concern for one's welfare."[4] In other words, although people are distinct individuals, in Japanese culture, it is generally best if they want the same thing. This deep level of sharing underpins the desire for harmony in interpersonal relations and the consideration of other member of the group.

40

According to Joy Hendry, *wa* is sometimes used to stand for Japan or Japaneseness.[5] In this context of *wa*, most Japanese might feel that if they become a Christian they will relinquish some of their 'Japaneseness' and abandon the group *wa*. Christians can be perceived as being antisocial and selfish because they disrupt the harmony of the family unit by refusing to observe many traditional Shinto and Buddhist rituals, especially those involving praying to spirits and reverencing the dead.[6]

The root of corporatism is found in the concept of *wa* or harmony. In contrast to individualism in the West, Japanese social life is based on corporatism driven by *wa*. Japanese culture and social life are both centered on this concept of harmony with others, both the living and deceased; harmony with gods as well as with nature is central here. Generally, the Japanese do not distinguish between the human and the divine or between the living and the dead. As Anthony Failow wrote in the Washington Post:

> In Japan, *wa* surrounds you. You can feel it in the priciest sushi bars and lowliest noodle parlors. Call it the particular Japanese way of looking at the world: of harmony, of collectiveness with do-not-rock-the-boat spirit. In the mythology of the 'Star wars movies, the *wa* is like the Force. To mess with the *wa* is a cardinal sin.[7]

The concept of *wa* was adapted in Japan's first constitution called *Prince Shotoku's Seventeen Article Constitution or Jushichijo Kenpo* and promulgated by Prince Shotoku in 604.[8] In Japan, group harmony means that a person knows his/her place in the social hierarchy and behaves accordingly. It also means that one has to keep silent even if one is unhappy or upset about something, just for the sake of not disturbing the harmony or *wa*. *Wa* tends to take precedence over individual autonomy, and self-reliance is recognized as a virtue only insofar as it aids in the creation of social harmony.[9] Mullins writes:

> In the Japanese context, Christianity and many new religions encourage individuals to consider alternative interpretations of reality, lifestyles, and spiritual disciplines. As a result, these new traditions can cause conflict and division in many situations and be disruptive of the *wa*, or harmony, of traditional Japanese society.[10]

During his presentation at the 2010 Tokyo Global Mission Consultation, Minoru Okuyama, the director of the Missionary Training Center in Japan, stated that the Japanese are afraid of disturbing the human relationships within their families or neighborhoods by becoming Christian. Okuyama emphasized that one of the most important things in Japan is *wa*— those who disturb it are regarded as bad, irrespective of whether they are right or wrong.[11] Therefore, it is quite hard for a Japanese to decide to become a Christian, for his/her choice means disturbing that harmony. There is a saying in Japanese, *deru kugi wa utareru*, which means "the protruding nail will be hammered down."[12] This illustrates very well how individuals are trained from an early age. Disturbing the group by being too individualistic or out of step with others is considered selfish.

Further, I understand *wa* to be operative in two major spheres of Japanese life: the private sphere (e.g., family) and the public sphere (e.g., neighborhood, employment, and education). In the latter, several concepts come into play, namely, those of inside and outside *(uchi–soto)*, social reciprocity *(giri)*, or one's inner and outer feelings or ideas *(honne–tatemae)*, benevolence *(amae)*, the personal view versus the group view, and also the view on truth and absolutism. Below, I describe these and their relation to *wa*.

3.1.2 Uchi–Soto

If we are to understand the concept of corporatism, we cannot avoid the Japanese cultural concept of *uchi–soto*. Japanese culture divides social life into two groups: *uchi,* an inner group to which the person belongs, and *soto*, which refers to everyone who is not in the *uchi* group.[13] The relationship between *uchi* and *soto* is complex since neither remains static; they can overlap and vary with time as a person's situation changes. *Uchi–soto* groups may be conceptualized as a series of overlapping circles. A person's position within a group and his or her relationship with other groups depends on context, situation, and period of life.[14] Children learn to distinguish between *uchi* and *soto* at an early age; for example, a child's house, class, or school is considered *uchi* depending on the situation.

The Japanese clearly distinguish insiders from outsiders in daily life based on *uchi* or *soto*. This concept has greatly influenced Japanese society, especially in the area of human relations. It promotes group consciousness. Groups are very vital since Japanese society is not individualistic and disturbing a group can be considered inappropriate and impolite.[15] For instance, students generally do not ask questions of their teachers in the classroom for fear of being viewed as individualistic, egoistic and childish *(wagamama)*.[16] Also, a company employee who is ambitious and seeks to move up the corporate ladder might be considered egoistic and childish. This is because that person disregards the group or *uchi* for the sake of personal interest. In Japan, it is vital to use suitable etiquette in social interaction and to behave appropriately. To do this, one must first assess a situation correctly, taking note of the status of the other party in particular. Is he or she *uchi* or *soto*?

According to Chie Nakane, once a person belongs to a group, it is important that they do not change groups too often. If they do, their loyalty will be questioned.[17] This may even be the case for most companies. They hesitate to employ people who are active members of a religious group because it is thought that since they are already a committed member of a religious group they will not be completely devoted to the company, it being considered an *uchi* group.

Thus, succinctly stated, *uchi-soto* can prevent most Japanese from accepting Christianity. It is considered the religion of soto, a Western religion for foreigners *(gaijin)* introduced to Japan by Western missionaries and it can eventually pose a threat to existing *uchi* groups. Belonging to the *uchi* group makes it hard for people to choose a new lifestyle. Devoting themselves to Christianity will mean that they disturb or even break the *wa* of their own group.

3.1.3 Giri

The term *giri* describes Japanese social and ethical obligations within a group. It is the obligation that defines and maintains the group harmony *(wa)*. Davies and Ikeno state that *giri* is "a key concept in understanding Japanese culture and certain characteristic patterns of behavior among the Japanese arising from traditional attitudes toward moral duty and social obligation."[18]

Giri refers to the obligation that one person has toward another in the community or group. Everybody in Japanese society has some form of *giri*. *Giri* depends on two important factors: a person (including their function or position) and the situation in which he or she is involved at a certain time and place.

Giri defines various relationships, including student/master and employee/employer. It operates both vertically and horizontally in a hierarchy and requires fulfillment of various expectations and carrying out of certain duties. Failing to perform these duties causes that person to lose face and brings shame and disgrace on himself/herself and the community.[19]

Since a *giri* relationship involves the continual creation of new duties and expectations, it can be prolonged indefinitely. *Giri* is not a special form of material consideration, but more of an affectively oriented duty. People in Japan are expected to express some affection toward others even if it does not come from the heart *(honne–tatemae)*. *Giri* is therefore strongly influenced by the hierarchical consciousness of the participants.[20]

Finally, breaking *giri,* means neglecting to honor the reciprocity toward a group as well as toward the ancestors. *Giri* involves ones obligation to participate in various rituals related to ancestors, festivals and other annual events. When a person chooses to become a Christian, it makes him/her appear to have broken the reciprocity and abrogated social, cultural responsibilities, all of which disturb *wa*. Thus, if the Japanese are given the opportunity to practice Christianity and at the same time to fulfill their *giri,* acceptance of Christianity would be much easier. On the other hand, Christians, especially Western Christians, may consider this to be a form of syncretism.

3.1.4 Honne–Tatemae

If harmony *(wa)* within a group or *uchi* is to be maintained, the expression of individual feelings or the dominance of others by imposing one's own opinion must be suppressed. The Japanese have a special concept in their culture for this: *honne–tatemae.* *Honne* means 'informal, personal reality in disregard of social parameters', while *tatemae* means 'official, public and socially required or politically correct.' *Honne* is an opinion or an action motivated by a person's true inner feelings, whereas *tatemae* is an opinion or action influenced by social norms. Thus, *honne* refers to a person's deep beliefs or intentions, while *tatemae* refers to socially attuned motives or intentions as these are shaped, encouraged, or suppressed by the norms of the majority.[21] These two concepts are often considered dichotomous. They reflect a contrast between genuinely held personal feelings and convictions and those that are socially controlled. Another dimension of this dichotomy is that *honne* is expressed privately, while *tatemae* may be openly professed.

In the formalities of a business meeting, the Japanese businessman tends to follow protocol. Later, while enjoying conversation with his colleagues over a glass of beer or *sake*, the same person will frankly express his *honne* regarding the issues raised at the meeting. With the aim of ensuring peace and harmony, the public self avoids confrontation, whereas the private self tends toward sincere self-expression.[22]

When trying to understand *honne* and *tatemae* and the way in which these contrasting concepts function in Japan, it is worthwhile to examine certain cultural characteristics such as the dislike of directly expressing opinions for fear that it might hurt the feelings of others and the importance of harmony and ceremony. Japanese people are usually careful about what they say and they often use *tatemae* in order to get along well with others.[23]

For example, when a person is visiting someone's home in Japan and it comes time for supper, people will often say, "Won't you dine with us?" However, this is not really an invitation; rather it is a subtle hint that it is time to go home. To people from other countries this may sound confusing, but for the Japanese it is a natural way to interact. So, the correct response to, "Won't you dine with us?" is "Thank you very much, but I am not hungry." This type of behavior is formulaic in Japanese society.[24]

Honne/tatemae forces most Japanese people to keep their worldview or religious beliefs to themselves. Consequently, they do not easily share them with others. When it comes to becoming a Christian, one has to keep one's convictions to oneself *(tatemae)* in order to maintain the group/social harmony *(wa)* or not disturb

47

the *wa* of other groups. Of course, this does not make the work of evangelism easy. Christians tend to want to share gospel openly with others, even when it disturbs, hinders or challenges the cultural and religious status quo as this is defined by fixed rules.

3.1.5 Amae

Amae, which can be roughly translated as dependence on the benevolence of others, is key to understanding the Japanese personality within a group/community to which a person belongs *(uchi)*. It is vital for getting along with others in Japan and is the basis for maintaining harmonious relationships *(wa)* in which children depend on their parents, younger people rely on their elders, grandparents depend on their adult children, and so on.[25]

The concept of *amae* greatly affects all aspects of Japanese life because it is connected to concepts such as *giri*. It makes it difficult for Japanese to say "no" to something or to directly reject or disagree with someone. People hesitate to refuse to engage with others for fear of breaking the relationship, offending that person, or hurting their feelings.[26] *Amae* is meant to create deep emotional bonds with others in the group, but it also creates distance from others outside the group. By becoming a Christian or committing to any other non-indigenous religion, a person may disturb or violate the deep emotional bonds that define the various groups to which they belong. This gives an entirely new and different dimension to the problem of Japanese conversion to Christianity.

3.2 Religious Aspects of Life in Japan

As mentioned in chapter one, the concept of *wa* is also found in the way the Japanese view religion. Harmony is not sought only in social relationships, but also between religions. The concept of *wa* does not promote exclusivity of religions or dominance of one over another; rather it supports harmony, co-existence and inclusivity. In fact the *wa* article issued by Prince Shotoku's constitution in 604 was intended to harmonize the relationship between Shintoism, Buddhism, and Confucianism.[27]

Japanese people tend to view all religious traditions within a more comprehensive category that is more generally termed "religion", rather than by focusing on distinct "religions" per se. It is often said that the Japanese are born Shinto, have a Christian (Western) style of wedding, and die Buddhist (many Japanese have Buddhist funerals). Further evidence that these different traditions are not clearly distinguished in Japan can be found in the fact that people do not feel compelled to commit to any particular organized religion. This mindset is called *mushukyo* in Japanese. It means "no religion" or "non-religious."[28] When a Japanese person talks about religion, he/she generally means revealed religions, particularly Christianity.[29] Thus, when Japanese people say that they are non-religious, most of them mean they are not committed to a revealed religion or religious organization.[30]

It is crucial to understand the characteristics of *mushukyo*. First, being non-religious does not mean that one does not participate in rituals related to gods, but rather that one does not identify him/herself as a member of one particular religious group. According to Mullins, the majority of Japanese continue to participate in household and institutional rituals, festivals, and annual events, and many hold what most observers would regard as "religious" beliefs (related to Buddhas, ancestors, gods, protective deities, and vengeful spirits). Thus, Mullins concludes that it would be a mistake to interpret *mushukyo* as meaning "non-religious" or "secular."[31]

For most Japanese, religion is understood in a Western–Christian framework, and thus folkloric or indigenous festivals known as *matsuri,* which are related to Shinto and sometimes to Buddhist traditions, are not considered to be religious.[32] This makes the Japanese religious mind still more complex and difficult to understand for outsiders. It is better understood, however, if we distinguish between religion and religious tradition. Japanese can participate in a religious tradition without being a part of an organized, revealed religion. To a certain degree, this can be true in Western European societies as well. For instance, one may celebrate Christmas in many Western countries without being religious or belonging to an organized church. Pentecost is a national holiday in the Netherlands; some people celebrate this event without being a part of a church or Christian denomination. Some may not even know what the meaning of the day actually is.

Further, *mushukyo* does not mean that the Japanese do not have religious sentiments. This is evident from the way they honor their ancestors during the *obon* season in mid-August or visit Shinto shrines and temples during the New Year. They are quite engaged when it comes to the expression of religious sentiment and even superstitions.

There are several motives why they do not choose to be a part of organized Christianity. According to Ama, annual events such as *obon* and other cultural festivals are a means of gaining spiritual peace and they replace the need for Western-style organized religion. There is thus no need for people to choose revealed religions as their means of spiritual liberation.[33] Another reason he cites has to do with various incidents and scandals surrounding religious organizations. These further contribute to the unpopularity of organized religions. Reports that some religious groups deceive their members into making large donations and organize seemingly supernatural events make most Japanese uncomfortable with organized religions.[34]

Another reason why they may feel suspicious about organized religions is the widely held perception that such religions are detrimental to the public peace. For instance, Japanese disapprove of Christians who walk in the streets with megaphones calling people sinners and asking them to repent. This is not acceptable to most of them.[35] Even though most Christians do not perform such acts, Japanese people are often cautious of Christianity because of its evangelical activities.[36]

Lastly, the exclusivist nature of some aspects of revealed religions also causes people to shun them. While those who are already members of a religion may enjoy reading holy texts, praying, and singing songs, these are often not pleasant experiences for an outsider. As Ama states, unless one becomes aware of the importance of life and its related anxieties, revealed religion does not make sense. This awareness is often created when one realizes how irrational life can be; it can lead a person to seek answers in revealed religions, but the Japanese generally prefer to be *mushukyo*.[37]

3.2.1 Non-Absolutism

According to Noriyuki Miyake, one of the reasons why most Japanese people are not Christians has to do with their views on the concept of absoluteness. Generally, they cannot understand the basics of the biblical faith because they are polytheists and tend to deny any type of absolute[38]— they view truth in relative terms. For them, truth is often understood in relation to the context in which it is experienced. This tendency to reject absolutism has its roots in the concept of *wa*, for in Japan maintaining and strengthening relationships between individuals is considered a sacred goal in itself. Nothing should be allowed to disrupt this harmony and any individual or institution that claims absolutism disturbs it.[39] In other words, the only concept that the Japanese take to be absolute is the all-inclusive harmony between individuals, ancestors, gods and nature, both supernatural as well natural. Fukuda describes this as follows:

> Many Japanese do not by any means recognize the existence of an absolute state isolated from environmental phenomena because, according to them, the phenomenal environment, whether made out of things visible or invisible, is itself the absolute.[40]

He goes on to use the term "Japanese religions" and thus to suggest that religion in Japan cannot be understood simply by separating it into individual components. It is therefore not farfetched to say that the names 'Shinto' and 'Buddhism' etc. express different facets of a single, syncretized Japanese religion.[41]

In particular, the concept of non-absolutism has consequences for the way Japanese people view Christianity. First, they do not take one particular religion to be absolute. Second, they tend not to view one specific God as absolute. Third, they view religion as a participatory means of securing harmony rather than as a set of personal beliefs in a fixed set of teachings. In what follows, I discuss each of these.

3.2.1.1 *Religion as Non-Absolute*
Japan is the host culture for various religious traditions. Even though the nation has gone through various religious conflicts in the course of its history, multiple religions have managed to co-exist there for centuries. The Japanese religious context can therefore be described as pluralistic. Robert Lee outlines the various aspects of this pluralism as follows:

> 1. *A nativistic element* in Shinto and emperor system.
> In the Meiji era the family, community society and nation were unified by an imperial ideology supported by State Shinto which, although modified today, continues to provide the Japanese their national identity.

2. *A Chinese component* in Confucian ethics and the family system. Since the Meiji era the traditional social ethic of Confucian loyalty and filial piety of former elite (samurai) class has become universalized as normative social identity for all Japanese.

3. *An Indian element* in a Buddhist religion that has been transformed into a Japanese Buddhism. Since the Kamakura era Buddhism has served as the religious dimension of Japanese life that deals with the problems of death and transiency.

4. *The indigenous "new religions"* and the "neo-new religions." These new religions, based upon Shinto or Nichiren Buddhism, have become for many the religious response to alienation caused by rapid modernization and the way for social reintegration into contemporary society.

5. *Western, largely secular, values* rising from Japan's rapid and highly successful modernization.

6. *A Cultural Christianity* that represents a borrowing of Western culture as popularized in Christmas celebrations and Christian-styles weddings.[42]

Mullins suggests the pluralism discussed above (i.e., the

co-existence of multiple religious traditions) has long characterized Japanese religion. The process of pluralization was enhanced from the nineteenth century onward with the emergence of many new religious movements and the transplantation of diverse forms of Christianity into the country from the West. Mullins speaks of serious discrepancies between the membership statistics claimed by these institutions and the self-understanding of the vast majority of Japanese:

> For example, Shinto institutions claim nearly 107 million adherents, while Buddhist institutions report a total of over 89 million followers. Combined with the number of adherents claimed by New Religions and Christian churches, the total exceeds the population of Japan (128 million) by some 82 million people. It is obvious many people are counted more than once as members of different religious institutions. Survey research, however, reveals that fewer than 10 percent of the population claim that they "belong" to a religious organization of any kind. This gap between institutional statistics and self-perception reinforces the widely held view that the figures provided by institutions are totally unreliable, but it remains a fact that many Japanese are at least loosely affiliated with more than one religious institution and participate in practices associated with multiple religious traditions.[43]

The idea that the Japanese are reluctant to accept one religion goes back to their encounter with Buddhism in the sixth century. According to Davies and Ikeno, during that period, the Japanese people noticed that if they chose to believe in Buddhism, then the emperor system would be abrogated, as would Shinto. It was through Shinto myths that the emperor's family was able to maintain its status in Japan. Thus, in the seventh century, as mentioned earlier, Prince Shotoku, who was the nephew of Emperor Suiko, occupied the regency and discovered a way of permitting Buddhism and the imperial system to co-exist along with another ethical system adopted from China, namely, Confucianism. As he stated, "Shinto is the trunk, Buddhism is the branches, and Confucianism is the leaves."[44] This approach enabled the Japanese to accept these new religions and ideologies, in this case Buddhism and Confucianism, in such a way as to avoid theoretical contradictions, because they were all seen as reconcilable. Davies and Ikeno suggest that the choice for co-existence had a great impact on the Japanese mentality and the way they view the world. Not only were they able to accept culture from other countries without any religious prejudices, but also they developed the habit of adopting only the most useful borrowings from other nations, cultures and religions and blending them into something uniquely Japanese.[45] This process is normally called *iitoko-dori*.

Iitoko-dori is widespread in Japan. It is the process of accepting convenient parts, however different and sometimes contradictory, of a religious value system.[46] *Iitoko-dori* was originally meant to maintain the wa between different religions, and their adherents as well as with the Japanese imperial system. For after the introduction of Buddhism to Japan, observing either Shinto or Buddhism exclusively could cause social and political unrest—disturbance of the *wa*. In other words, when one religion supersedes another, it disturbs existing relationships and introduces ambiguity into social reciprocities and duties.

When Christianity was introduced in Japan, people were initially open to its precepts provided that they would not disturb the existing *wa,* which was the result of the centuries-old *iitoko-dori*. The arrival of Christianity did, however, disturb the *wa* in various ways. First, it contributed to the ongoing conflicts between various *daimyos,* since Japan was experiencing national unrest. Further, it did not genuinely respect the centuries-old Japanese imperial system, and after the occupation by the Allied forces in 1945, that system was forcibly reduced more or less to a Western form of monarchy, (see chapter seven).

It is obvious that throughout Japanese history, Christianity did not and could not successfully contribute to the *wa* or participate in *iitoko-dori*. The main reason for this is its embrace of absolutism. According to Davies and Ikeno, Christians have an absolute sense of values and this is the basis for their life decisions. Yet, the Japanese sense of ethical values is relative. It varies with people's opinions and with the contexts in which decisions have to be made. Their long history of *iitoko-dori* makes it possible for the Japanese to change their sense of values in a short time and with little difficulty[47] as long as *wa* is maintained.

3.2.1.2 *The Absolute God*

Since the Japanese value harmony and truth understood in social context more than they do absolute truth, the concept of an absolute God as presented by Christianity is hard to understand or accept. First, let us briefly look at the concept of God in Japanese culture.

In Japanese, god or gods are called *kami*. They are the Shinto deities. However, they bear little resemblance to the gods of the monotheistic religions. They are shadowy, formless entities —or people's projections—that are largely devoid of personality and resemble impersonal manifestations of power. Further, in Japanese culture *kami* have never been considered absolute or transcendent in relation to man and the world. Hence, there is a significant continuity between the various *kami*. In sharp contrast to the symbolic dichotomy between the creator and creation in Western religions, the relationship between *kami* and man is well symbolized by the term *oyako*, an expression specifying the parent–child, or better, the ancestor–descendant relation.[48]

The Japanese thinking about the *kami* has also changed in numerous ways during the course of history. In ancient times, Japan was influenced by Chinese and Korean culture and, to a lesser degree, by India via China. As a result, the concepts of the Buddha, of deities, and of a heaven, as these existed in Buddhism, Taoism and Confucianism, have strongly influenced the Japanese concept of *kami*.[49] In the sixteenth and seventeenth centuries, and again in the second half of the nineteenth century, Japan was also influenced by the Christian idea of God.

Catholic orders such as the Jesuits came to Japan in the sixteenth and seventeenth centuries, transmitting to them a *bona fide* monotheism. After a more than two hundred year long governmentally imposed ban on Christianity, many Protestant and Catholic missionaries, mostly from the USA, returned to Japan. So, the Japanese began to deal with the newly introduced idea of God and find a way of understanding it spiritually. Considering this historical process, it is quite natural that the ancient concept of *kami* has changed considerably over time and become ever more complicated in modern society.[50]

All *kami* are considered to have superior knowledge and power; they hold within their power those areas of life that are beyond human control. They have no shape of their own. If they are to manifest themselves, they must be summoned or cajoled into a vessel of suitable form. These vessels are known as *yorishiro* and are frequently long and thin: trees, wands, banners, or long stones are common.[51] Dolls are also believed to be the residence of *kami*. Also, certain physically gifted people can act as mediums between humans and *kami*. They are usually women; a *kami* may borrow a women's body to communicate and reveal things.

The *kami* are inherently amoral. They are simply powers that respond favorably or unfavorably to the human community according to the treatment they receive. If we treat them well by performing the proper rituals, offerings, and cultic worship, they can be expected to respond with blessings in the form of good rice harvests, flourishing progeny, and protection from fire, famine, and disease.[52]

59

Most Japanese do not consider God to be absolute or one, nor do they view him as the creator of both nature and human beings. *Kami* do not have creative powers as does the God of Christianity; in other words, they are not thought to have created the heavens and the earth and everything in them, living or dead. In Christianity, by contrast, God is not a part of the created world. People can only know about God by manifestations of God in the world. Thus, the act of creation and the created world separate man from God.[53]

Further, in Japan human beings can become gods themselves or others can recognize them as *kami.* In other words, human beings have the ability to appoint and recognize other humans as gods. This contradicts the Christian view that God alone is the creator of all beings. For the Japanese, human beings can also become *kami* after their death and continue to exert an influence on this world, generally through the continuation of the qualities that marked them out in this life. The living can create *kami*, or they can recognize that the importance of particular individuals is such that they should be recognized after death (or even occasionally when still alive) as *kami.*[54]

Lastly, the concept of *kami* is in alignment with the concept of harmony *(wa).* Reid describes *kami* as "divine beings more immanent than transcendent, who desire to see their people enjoying a life of communal harmony and abundance, filled with dynamic vitality and purity of heart."[55] In order to achieve this communal harmony, gods and people have to make concessions by refusing absolutism and accepting relativism. For instance:

Shinto scholar Ueda Kenji (1927–2003) criticizes the
Western view on the concept of God. Kenji suggests
that *kami* is an existence that cannot be understood
by human reason, as westerners tend to do. Instead,
from the Shinto perspective, Japanese *kami* are
considered as a life force within all beings. Every
being has an individual *kami* nature deeply hidden
inside. *Kami* is not regarded as a particular being
but as a force. It is the force of life that constitutes
beings as such. In the Japanese tradition, people
are not particularly concerned about the concept of
kami; they regard the experience of *kami* as more
important than doctrines.[56]

The non-absolute view of God has several consequences. First, no
one god has absolute power and authority over any others. Unlike
the Christian God, the Japanese gods do not, in and of themselves,
represent a religion that people are to believe in. Therefore, there
should be harmony not only between people and gods but also
among the different gods. This is evident in the way Shinto and
Buddhist concept of God has syncretized in Japan. Hasegawa states
that, in the late eighth century and with the support of the imperial
household, the Buddha was given an independent status socially
and politically equal to the *kami*.[57] The introduction of Buddhist
icons and statues transformed the concept of *kami* and, as a result,
the Japanese came to worship images of the *kami*. During the Heian
and Nara periods, Buddhist scholars introduced the theory of *honji-*

61

suijaku, according to which Buddhas appeared in the world *(honji)*
in the shape of *kami* for the purpose of saving people. Ise-shinto,
however, proposed an opposing theory: Shinto gods were the *honji*
and the Buddha, the *suijaku.* This theory was called *han-honji suijaku
setsu (anti honji suijaku).*[58]

Gradually, the Buddha came to be accepted in Japan and
took the form of *kami* in the Japanese indigenous faith. Buddhism
was therefore adopted into Japanese society in a transformed way.
Eventually, both Buddha and *kami* came to be regarded as one, and
the unity of all of them was named *dainichi.*[59] Further information
on *dainichi* and its relationship to Christian theology is provided in
chapter four.

Second, unlike the Christian God who is considered to be
omnipotent and omniscience, the *kami* are limited to performing
specific functions. They *cannot* perform every sort of task and
do not know everything, but can only influence situations and
circumstances to a certain degree. Moreover, this can only happen
when they are being treated correctly. In the Christian view, God has
to be worshipped, whereas in Japanese culture, gods are meant to
be treated correctly. Treating the *kami* correctly is more important
than worshipping them. The Japanese culture, values, traditions,
rituals, ceremonies and festivals have all developed around this
notion of right treatment. All of these cultural institutions and
practices are required to ensure that the *kami* are pleased. I think it
is too simplistic to suggest that average Japanese are worshippers
of gods, when, in fact, they are mostly *"treat gods correctly type"* of
people.

This *"treat gods correctly"* view has two major underlying motives: fear and the hope of obtaining good luck. Often fear relates to provoking the anger or jealousy of the *kami* or disturbing the harmony between the individual or group and the *kami*. The latter can have consequences such as bad luck, bad fortune, illness, calamities or disasters both at the level of the individual and that of the group. The other motivating factor is that the Japanese like to ensure they have good luck, especially in times of need. The Japanese have a saying *kurushii toki no kamidanomi,* which means "turn to gods in times of trouble". School examinations, job interviews, university applications, and many other occasions are considered times of trouble.[60] According to Reader, the *kami* are available to be petitioned by those in need. Their existence is thus not so much a matter of cognitive belief but cultural acceptance and need: when the situation calls for it, the *kami* are there to perform the role ascribed to them. In other words, as Reader suggests, in general terms the Japanese religious world provides a psychological support system. It can be drawn upon when circumstances require it and it can provide answers and solutions when problems arise, yet these gods do not demand attention at other times. People may move into and out of modes of religiosity according to requirements and circumstances.[61]

In Shinto, the Japanese often use the word *suuhai* for "worship" in the term "ancestor worship," however *suuhai* has the slightly stronger meaning of adoration. This stands in contrast to the Christian concept of the worship of God. Offner argues that it is still more difficult to define the intentions of the individual who is the subject of words like *suuhai*. In his view, in fact, the individual would find it difficult to analyze his/her own feelings in this regard. It is therefore crucial to understand not only the words but also the emotions and motivations of the Japanese and to try not to impose Western Christian definitions and feelings upon Japanese words and actions.[62] Concerning the word *suuhai*, it is crucial to get beneath words to the attitudes they are meant to express. Offner suggests that since there is no transcendent absolute in the Japanese tradition, no being that demands the total commitment or wholehearted allegiance of humans, respect, honor, veneration and/ or worship may be accorded to the multitude of spirits, which are considered to be present in various forms.[63] Thus, when Christians speak of worshipping one absolute omnipotent and omniscient God, the Japanese may not be able to understand, accept or practice this.

Further, Japanese religious culture does not have any concept of a personal love toward the *kami*. Hence, when a Japanese is introduced for the first time to the concept of the Christian God, he/she may find this notion absurd. In keeping with what has been discussed above, the *kami* do not love people unconditionally. Hence, the concept of a loving God in the Christian sense is not easy for the Japanese to understand. Also to worship and love one absolute God and reject the *kami* and Japanese traditions means to abandon the *uchi, ie*-traditions, and *giri* to disharmonize the *wa* both with gods and ancestors and to disturb the social *wa*. The challenge then is how to bring the message of Christianity to a people who have such a complex way of looking at and practicing religion.

64

Notes

1   Gary B. Palmer, *Toward A Theory of Cultural Linguistics* (Austin:
University of Texas Press, 1996), 114.

2   Richard DeWitt, *Worldviews: An Introduction to the History and
Philosophy of Science* (Chichester: Wiley-Blackwell: 2010), 7.

3   Harold Perkin, *The Third Revolution: Professional Elites in the
Modern World* (New York: Routledge, 1996), 207.

4   Ibid.

5   Joy Hendry, *Understanding Japanese Society*, 3rd Edition
(New York: Taylor & Francis, 2003), 240.

6   Hendry, 139.

7   "Japanese Society: Wa, Confucianism, Homogeneity, Conformity,
Individualism and Hierarchies," last modified March 2012,
http://factsanddetails.com/japan.php?itemid=642&catid=18

8   The first article was as follows: Harmony should be valued and
quarrels should be avoided. Everyone has his biases, and few men
are far-sighted. Therefore some disobey their lords and fathers
and keep up feuds with their neighbors. But when the superiors are
in harmony with each other and the inferiors are friendly, then affairs
are discussed quietly and the right view of matters prevails.
http://www.sarudama.com/japanese_history/jushichijokenpo.shtml

9   Kenneth Dale, *Coping with Culture: The Current of the Japanese
Church* (Tokyo: Lutheran Booklets, No. 3, 1996), 29.

10   Mark R. Mullins, "The Social and Legal Status of Religious Minorities
     in Japan" (paper presented at International Coalition for Religious
     Freedom Conference on "Religious Freedom and the New
     Millennium", Tokyo, Louisiana, May 23–25, 1998).

11   Michelle A. VU, "Mission Leader: Why So Few Christians in Japan?"
     Christian Post Reporter, May 18, 2010. http://www.christianpost.
     com/news/mission-leaderwhy-so-few-christians-in-japan-45217/

12   Roger J. Davies and Osamu Ikeno, *The Japanese Mind:
     Understanding Contemporary Japanese Culture* (Boston: Tuttle
     Publishing, 2002) 53.

13   Davies and Ikeno, 217.

14   For example, a person will usually have a family, a job, and other
     groups or organizations to which they belong. Their position within
     the various groups and relationship with other groups will vary with
     the position they have at a given moment. Thus, a company
     employee may have a high position within the company but have a
     humble role in relation to the company's customers. The same
     employee may hold a black belt in karate giving them a superior
     position within their karate club, but they may be a beginner at
     tennis and thus occupy an inferior position in the tennis club,
     and so on.

15   Davies and Ikeno, 195.

16   Davies and Ikeno, 58.

17   Chie Nakane, *Japanese Society* (Berkley: University of Californian
     Press, 1970), 21.

18   Davies and Ikeno, 95.

19   Hendry, 240.

20   Ibid.

21   Davies and Ikeno, 115.

22   http://www.reachinginternationals.com/uploads/documents/
How_to_Share_the_Love_of_God_with_Japanese.pdf,17.

23   Davies and Ikeno, 116.

24   Ibid.

25   Davies and Ikeno, 17.

26   Davies and Ikeno, 19.

27   "Japanese Society: Wa, Confucianism, Homogeneity, Conformity,
Individualism and Hierarchies," last modified March 2012,
http://factsanddetails.com/japan.php?itemid=642&catid=18

28   Ibid.

29   Toshimaro Ama distinguishes two categories of religion in Japan:
revealed and natural religions. According to Ama Buddhism,
Judaism, Christianity, Islam, and some new religions are considered
revealed religions because they have specific books and scriptures
that provide guidelines for life and religious rituals. In contrast,
natural religions are more traditional and based on folklore; they
have few or no books or scriptures. Even though Shintoism does
have some texts and scriptures, it is considered to be more a
natural religion (Ama, 1).

30   Toshimaro Ama, *Why Are the Japanese Non-Religious? Japanese Spirituality Being Non-Religious in a Religious Culture* (Lanham: University Press of America, 2005),vii.

31   Mark R. Mullins, "Religion in Contemporary Japanese Lives," in *Routledge Handbook of Japanese Culture and Society,* ed. Victoria L. Bestor et al. (London: Routledge, 2011), 63.

32   Ama, 2.

33   Ama, 4.

34   Ama, 8.

35   Ibid.

36   Ibid.

37   Ama, 64.

38   Noriyuki Miyake, "A Challenge to Pentecostal Mission in Japan," *Asian Journal of Pentecostal Studies* 9:1(2006), 83–94, (88).

39   Fukuda, 52.

40   Ibid.

41   Fukuda, 45.

42   Lee, 68–69.

43   Mullins 2011, 65.

44   Davies and Ikeno, 128.

45   Ibid.

46   Davies and Ikeno, 129.

47   Davies and Ikeno, 130.

48   Noriyoshi Tamaru and David Reid (Eds.), *Religion in Japanese Culture: Where Living Traditions Meet a Changing World* (New York: Kodansha International, 1996), 16.

49   Nobutaka Inoue, "Perspectives Towards Understanding the Concept of Kami," in *Contemporary Papers on Japanese Religions*, online version (1988). http://www2.kokugakuin.ac.jp/ijcc/wp/cpjr/kami/inoue.html#tnotel

50   Ibid.

51   Richard Bowring and Peter Kornicki, *The Cambridge Encyclopedia of Japan* (Cambridge: Cambridge University Press, 1993), 152.

52   Bowring and Kornicki, 39.

53   Alexei Batchourine, "The Shinto Concept of Kami" Moscow State University, the Faculty of Philosophy http://trubnikovann.narod.ru/Bachessa.htm

54   Ian Reader, *Religion in Contemporary Japan* (Honolulu: University of Hawai Press, 1991), 25–26.

55   David Reid, *The Cultural Shaping of Japanese Christianity* (Berkeley: Asian Humanities Press, 1991), 5.

56   Emi Mase-Hasegawa, *Christ in Japanese Culture: Theological Themes in Shusaku Endo's Literary Works* (Leiden: Brill, 2008), 31.

57   Hasegawa, 32.

58   Hasegawa, 33.

59   Ibid.

60   Reader, 20.

61   Reader, 21-22.

62   Clark B. Offner, "A Foreign Christian's Struggle with Japanese Concepts of Respect, Honor, Veneration, Worship" Hayama Missionary Seminar Report 1988, PDF Version 1.1, November 2008, 74.

63   Offner, 75.

Chapter 4

THEOLOGICAL FACTORS

Prince Shotoku (574–622) stated that "Shinto is the trunk, Buddhism is the branches, and Confucianism is the leaves."[1] However, after Christianity was introduced in the late sixteenth century, it did not succeed in being added to the list of the religions mentioned here. If we attempt to revise Prince Shotoku's statement by adding Christianity, what would part of the tree would it represent? Or would it be accepted in the list anyway? If it had its way, would it uproot the trunk and establish another one with new branches and leaves?

Ichiro Hori suggests that Shinto, Buddhism and Confucianism fused so completely in Japan that they lost their original identities: Confucianism and Shinto have borrowed Buddhist metaphysics and psychology; Buddhism and Shinto have borrowed many aspects of Confucian ethics; and, perhaps most importantly, both Confucianism and Buddhism have become adapted into the indigenous religion of Japan instead of maintaining their uniqueness, even though they manifest themselves in many different forms and varieties.[2] In the past, Western Christianity has not been able to fully compromise its doctrines and traditions because of its fear of syncretism. Nor could it supplant Shinto, Buddhism or Confucianism. At the same time, Japan was not able to completely eradicate Christianity.

This chapter represents a search for theological factors as to why Christianity was/is not able to find its place in relation to

71

the three main religions of this country.[3] The clash between the Japanese worldview and that of Western Christianity has engendered a theological conflict. Topics such as Christ, sin, salvation, the infallibility of the Bible, life after death, and the Christian stand on ancestor worship, are just a few of the theological points that stand in contradiction to Japanese thinking. In the following paragraphs, I discuss these items and identify areas of conflict between the Christian message and Japanese religious views.

4.1 Original Sin, Man and Nature

In Christianity, according to the message that most missionaries preach, man is sinful by birth. This is the result of the original sin committed by Adam and Eve and transmitted to the rest of humanity. Already from birth, sin separates man from God. There is thus a continuity of sin in man.[4] Christians believe that it can be removed only when a person chooses to believe and worship Jesus Christ, the Son of God.[5] Even then, a regenerated human is still sinful and as long as he or she lives here on earth, the grace of God provides forgiveness for their sins until they die and enter paradise.

On the other hand, Christians view the created world as fallen—the earth was cursed as result of original sin. Thus, this world is to be renewed and restored to a certain degree by the children of God[6] (those who believe in Jesus Christ) until His second coming, when it will be eternally redeemed and renewed. This view of fallen man/nature has led Western Christianity to adopt a dualistic view of the world (e.g., good and evil, God and Satan, heaven and hell); this view is strongly influenced by Persian culture and Zoroastrianism.

72

In contrary to the Christian view, the concept of original sin is not found in Shinto. Man is considered to have a predominantly divine nature. There is a saying in Japan that "man is *kami's* (god's) child." This divinity in human nature makes us the carrier of a long, continuous history that comes down from ancestors and continues through descendants.[7] Man is also seen as a responsible constituent of various social groups. Such a view of humans places us in a spectrum of continuity and community insofar as it causes us to recognize that each man has an individual personality, but, at the same time, is not separate from others (community). This continuity and community are not only shared with others but also with nature and the environment. In Christianity, the continuity of the divine in man is interrupted: man, nature and God are all separated by sin. Western Christianity consequently promotes individualism: salvation occurs on an individual basis, being the result of personal choice. Most Japanese will not understand or agree when Christians or foreign missionaries in Japan suggest that man is a sinner by nature and that he needs Jesus to be restored.

The concept of continuity in Japanese culture, especially in Shinto, is also approached cyclically. In Shinto it is called *naka-ima* (i.e., "middle present" or "here and now"). *Naka-ima* is used to express the importance of the now, which is at one and the same time related to the past and future. Thus, the present moment is the very center of all conceivable times[8] and there is only constant repetition of historical pattern. That is to say, the Japanese do not have a linear conception of time nor a concomitant view of human progress; they have no notion of a beginning that started with a sin and an end that will permanently destroy sinful man and nature.

In the Japanese context, the notion of original sin is not taken literally and so not understood to be transferred to succeeding generations as a result of one man's choice. In contrast to this, most Evangelical missionaries acknowledge the sinfulness of man, as stated in Japan Evangelical Missionary Association's statement of faith.[9] Tokutaro Takakura (1885–1934) considers it to be a sort of super-historical truth in which "human nature" is essentially egoistic. He believes this is because "we cannot help but feel responsible for sin."[10] Takakura also points out that there is still a corporate solidarity of sin throughout human race, a fundamental problem of selfishness that transcends all humanity, throughout time, individually and corporately.[11]

According to Yoji Inoue, original sin does not mean something transmitted from Adam to the rest of humanity in the form of "the sins of the father are visited upon the child."[12] Original sin is rather already present in man—it does not have to be transmitted. By eating the "apple", we are "trying to be like God", in our everyday life. Inoue argues that the traditional expression "it came from Adam" only shows that our flaws are so deeply situated within us that we can do nothing to resolve them of our own accord. Original sin is more like the stain on our mind, because of which we cannot accept others as they are, be they human beings or nature itself.[13]

Inoue considers the story of Adam and Eve and original sin as a teaching for all mankind. Within us all, even in this modern age of technology, is a world of pandemonium and brutishness, the extent of which we cannot fully be aware.[14]

Kanzo Uchimura considered sin to be the absence of God in someone's life, the result of a choice to leave God:

> If goodness is to follow God, evil must be to leave God. Stealing, murder or adultery is sin not by itself, but by the result of leaving God. When I am condemned by law for murder, I am called upon not for violation of the homicide law itself but for leaving my God. I shall not commit a crime whatever tempted, or shall not even cherish an idea of sin, as long as God abides within me and I with Him. Defectiveness, contempt of others, desiring lust, arrogance, and neglecting my neighbors, all these result from leaving God. Consequently, I shall be able to do good only if I return to God. This indeed must be the only way to avoid sin.[15]

4.2 Sin and Japanese Culture

In the biblical context, sin is disobedience to God. It is transmitted to us through original sin as well as through the choices one makes in life, choices that place us in opposition to God. In Japanese culture, however, sin is viewed as a "disturbance" of the harmony *wa*. Anything that disturbs the harmony of the living with the ancestors, with nature, but especially with the group, is considered sinful. Political, social, and family regulations have become merged into a single all-embracing system in Japan. When one member of a family chooses to follow Jesus Christ, that person may disturb the overall harmony of the family if, for example, he or she refuses to attend family ceremonies. Family traditions are also thereby disturbed, as are the spirits of the ancestors. Also, such a person may choose not participate in neighborhood religious activities. This non-participation could bring shame and disgrace upon the rest of the family and so also disturb the harmony of the family with the neighborhood. Such choices and actions are considered equivalent to sin in the Japanese mind. Caldarola argues that in the Japanese mind, sin may mean directly causing some kind of trouble or discomfort to one's neighbor.[16]

Since in Japan, there is really no proper concept of sin as understood in Christianity, it is also difficult for most Japanese to understand the notion of God's forgiveness. Sin, crime, and bad manners overlap to some degree in practically any culture, but in Japan they are more clearly identified as being synonymous than elsewhere.[17] George Sansom suggests that *tsumi* is about doing things that are offensive to the gods. Uncleanness is one of the main tsumi. It may not, per se, be caused by what other religions would call moral guilt.[18] Uncleanness or impurity, *kegare*, can be caused by dirt, which has to be avoided. For instance, preparation of religious observances requires washing the body and putting on fresh garments.[19] Sexual intercourse, menstruation and childbirth were regarded as causes of ceremonial impurity, and they had to be removed by lustration, abstention, and prayer.

Also diseases, wounds, and death were viewed as sources of uncleanness. Sickness and all external signs of disease, such as sores, eruptions, and discharges, were also held to be defilements.

76

Thus, it is pollution that has to be washed away and not moral guilt or sin.[20] In contrast, in Christianity cleanliness and uncleanliness have moral overtones based on Jesus Christ's words, "What goes into a man's mouth does not make him 'unclean,' but what comes out of his mouth, that is what makes him 'unclean.'"[21] Thus, Makito Nagasawa suggests that Protestant Christians in Japan are more apt to be concerned with spiritual purification and to stay away from worldly affairs. For them, what outwardly differentiates Christians from non-Christians is habits such as not smoking and not drinking. With their pietistic mentality, argues Nagasawa, they focus on an awareness of sin and guilt as a condition of genuine sanctification. They are always aware of the inner conflict between Christian values and those of the secular and pagan society.[22] Uncleanliness can easily be "washed away" by a prayer or a ceremony. Thus, in the eyes of most Japanese salvation and forgiveness of sins are not needed, as ceremonies or prayers can wash away any uncleanliness.

Another aspect of *tsumi* is that it is the word used for "crime". Based on this definition, only criminals, thieves, and killers are sinners. Thus, an average Japanese person does not consider himself or herself a sinner in the sense of being a criminal. Generally, in Christianity, sin is viewed as disobeying the Lord's commands and rejecting God's Son Jesus Christ as Lord and Savior. But, the Japanese people think of sin in synthetic terms, as something that defies the laws of the land.

Some missionaries suggest that the Christian concept of sin may be best communicated through the related notions of guilt and shame. Japanese society is not solely shame oriented, as some classic anthropologists like Ruth Benedict have suggested—it is also guilt oriented. David Lewis proposes that Japanese culture exhibits both orientations.[23] He advises missionaries to use the Japanese word *ryoshin,* a reference to guilt, instead of *tsumi,* which implies sin. According to Lewis, *ryoshin* is an indigenous and universally understood concept.[24] In order to communicate the gospel, missionaries need to address their message to the voice of conscience that already exists within the Japanese culture. Rather than espousing "foreign" values, the Christian gospel in Japan should address what is already recognized by the people themselves as areas of moral failure and guilt. In this way the "inner" voice of "conscience" can be made to accord with the outer voice of the Christian who is seeking to communicate the gospel.[25] Lewis conducted research among the Japanese people on what they consider as shameful and what they feel guilty about. Approximately 660 people were questioned. Stealing (99.1%), lying (94.7%), and betrayal of one's group (93.5%) were the top three acts that caused respondents to experience feelings of shame.[26] The following acts were the top three in terms of engendering as sense of guilt: stealing (98.6%), not repaying a debt (96.8%) and betrayal of one's group (94.8%).[27]

Lewis' research shows that the Japanese do have a sense of shame and guilt, especially when they feel that they have violated group loyalty, which is, of course, connected to group harmony. On the other hand, his research also indicates that the Japanese do have a high standard of morality. The only formal difference is that they do not relate this to the great fall and the fundamental nature of humankind. Even though the shame–guilt concept might seem a better alternative for conveying the Christian concept of sin in Japan, it still causes some complications. For instance in Eastern cultures (particularly in Japanese culture), it is not polite to straightforwardly speak about someone's shame and guilt.

Shusaku Endo (1923–1996) has yet a different understanding of sin. He distinguishes it from evil. In his novel, *Silence*, (1969) Endo states, "… sin, is not what it is usually thought to be; it is not to steal and tell lies. Sin is for one man to walk brutally over the life of another, and to be quite oblivious or mindless of the wounds he has left behind."[28] In his view, one can describe sin as something deeper, which Endo calls evil. Evil is perpetrated when people stop thinking and become mindless, distracted by pride, or even fooled by false humility. They forget things, and fail to consider both themselves and others. Such forgetfulness is the source of all human sorrow, even wars. Mindlessness creates the atmosphere in which evil thrives.[29] Sin in the Japanese context (i.e., crime) will be forgiven if one acknowledges it and either asks for forgiveness or pays the necessary price. But there also exists a subconscious evil. It is an inevitable violent emotion that makes one fall to extreme depths of depravity.[30] According to Endo, Jesus did not die for human sins. His death was unnecessary unless it was for something more fearful than sin. Evil can be called a "black hole" that humans cannot resist falling into; Jesus died to save us from this.[31]

In short, as indicated above, the concept of sin in Japanese thought runs contrary to the Christian concept. Most Japanese view it in ethical terms, whereas Christians understand it not only in

79

ethical terms but also in spiritual and supernatural ones. Caldarola indicates that this feeling of uneasiness with the supernatural experience of sin and atonement echoes the cultural shock commonly experienced by Japanese who come into contact with Christianity. It also accounts for one of the most serious difficulties in the acculturation of Christianity in Japan.[32]

4.3 Salvation in Japanese Context

Perceptions of sin have implications for the way one views salvation and life after death. Generally, in Christianity, salvation comes through a personal belief in Jesus Christ who reconciles man to God the Father through His sacrifice on the cross. Those who choose to believe in atonement through Christ obtain the gift of eternal life in paradise or heaven. In addition to this, within some church traditions, it is believed that salvation is connected to membership in the Church, because the Church is the administrator of the sacrament of atonement. Thus, outside the Church there may be no salvation. Since the Japanese do not consider sin to be a crime against the supreme God, their idea of salvation does indeed differ from that of Christians.

In Japanese, the word *harai* is used for salvation. It means purity, purification, attainment, or enlightenment. Generally, in Japan, salvation can be analyzed from both Buddhist and Shinto perspectives. In Shinto, it is more or less about being free from uncleanliness, whereas in Japanese Buddhism it equates to enlightenment. Inagaki and Jennings suggest "that Buddhism connects human salvation with the idea of *nirvana, sunyata* (emptiness) enlightenment, self-awareness or absolute nothingness. The person who has experienced nirvana sees the world in a new way, because he has experienced a kind of regeneration."[33] In fact, a notion equivalent to salvation through transcendence was introduced to Japan via Buddhism in the twelfth century during the Kamakura era (1185-1333). According to Inagaki and Jennings, Buddhism offered something unique to the masses for the first time, something that had not been present in Japanese culture before—a teaching of 'salvation' based on transcendence. It was Pure Land Buddhism and Zen Buddhism in particular that lent a depth dimension to the Japanese culture.[34] Of course, there are various interpretations of salvation within Japanese Buddhism. For instance the *Jodo-Shin* School of the Pure Land believes that good works and mercy received by calling Amida's name bring salvation. However, the *Jodo-Shin-Shu* of the True Sect of Pure Land, school of Shinran believes that salvation comes totally from "beyond", from outside ourselves.[35] Uchimura described the differences between the concepts of salvation as taught by Amida Buddhism and Christianity. He noted that the former simply speaks of mercy *(jihi)* given by a benevolent Buddha as a way to salvation, whereas the latter goes further by emphasizing the concept of *(gi)* the human sense of justice; before God pours out His mercy, humans have to be made just in His eyes.[36]

As noted above, salvation in Shinto is understood as a form of purification. This makes the need for ceremonies and rites even more crucial. Salvation is therefore understood in more or less earthly terms and in the context of human achievement. Prosperity and health are also aspects of salvation. In this case, performing rituals and traditions, keeping the ancestors happy, and satisfying the regional, seasonal or family gods are all part of the path to salvation. In short, treating the *kami* and ancestors correctly leads to salvation. For this, purification rites and ceremonies are requisite. Still, the Japanese general public does not have a distinct concept of salvation, but rather one that is a mixture of Shinto and Buddhist precepts.

Generally speaking, in Christianity, there are also various ideas about, and ways of interpreting, the concept of salvation. However, they all share one thing is common: salvation and access to heaven are obtained through Jesus Christ by believing in him and they are by grace. At the same time, in Christianity, salvation can also mean the restoration of a personal relationship with God. There are also denominations that relate salvation to membership of a particular church. These Christian ideas of salvation considered together— namely, salvation only through Jesus Christ,[37] only through the Christian religion, exclusive paradise for Christians and salvation through the church — I term as "exclusive salvation". As the term itself indicates, this is a salvation for Christians only. This too has negative consequences for the acceptance of Christianity by the Japanese. I here explain some aspects of these concepts and discuss some of the consequences of their acceptance.

4.3.1 Salvation only through Christianity

As described in the previous chapter, Japanese culture is more or less driven by inclusivity. From the outset, therefore, an exclusive concept of God is not easily accepted, let alone that of an exclusive savior,

Jesus Christ. Jesus may be considered a wise man, an enlightened individual, a Buddha who may bring illumination to others, but it doesn't mean that he is the only Buddha through whom salvation and access to paradise can come.

According to Joy Hendry; one of the problems for Christianity in Japan is the exclusive nature of the religion.[38] Christianity does not tolerate the inclusion of other religions within it and does not accept any other path to salvation (prophets, the Buddha or other religions). Even salvation defined in terms of present benefits (i.e., happiness and prosperity) can come only through Jesus Christ for Christians— any other form of these things may be false or temporary. And, given such a doctrinal framework it is hard, indeed well-nigh impossible, for Christianity to accept any other religion or belief system; at the same time, it is very difficult for the Japanese people to understand such ideas and situate them within their belief system.[39]

Japanese indigenous thinkers such as Kanzo Uchimura (1861–1930) and Katsumi Takizawa (1909–1984) attempted to address the problematic claim of salvation coming exclusively through Jesus Christ, but they were not applauded by the Japanese Christians for their thinking on this. Uchimura, for instance, wrote:

"Buddha is the Moon; Christ is the Sun.
Buddha is the Mother; Christ is the Father.
Buddha is Mercy, Christ is Righteousness . . .

I love the Moon and I love the night; but as the night
is far spent and the day is at hand, I now love the Sun

more than I love the Moon; and I know that the love of the Moon in included in the love of the Sun, and that he who loves the Sun loves the Moon also."[40]

And Takizawa wrote:

"When we see that the incarnation is one mythical idea applied to Jesus in order to express the experiential fact that Jesus is sufficient, effective contact point of salvation between God and us, we must not then draw the negative conclusion that Jesus alone is the unique, effective point of contact between God and humankind. Because we have found salvation through Christ we worship this Christ, but we must not therefore deny other contact points of salvation, which we hear from others. We do not denounce other roads of faith, but we can commend Christian faith. Even though we do not say that there is no salvation outside of Christ, we can speak about salvation through Christ." [41]

Takizawa's approach suits the Japanese social context with its emphasis on harmonious co-existence and inclusion without loss of basic identity. He does not deny the assurance of salvation through Christ, and also does not exclude other religious paths. And, he thereby avoids any conflict of ideas, as this is acceptable in Japanese culture. Just like Prince Shotoku, he welcomes co-existence and

84

mutual respect. Uchimura (the Buddha as the moon and Christ as the Sun), actually does more or less the same thing as Takizawa, namely to include the love of the Moon under the love of the Sun. Actually, he speaks about the light which is more important than either the Moon or the Sun. For light that streams from the Sun is also reflected from the Moon. The reflector may be different, but the light is the same.

Inclusionism may tend toward syncretism, as some evangelical missionaries might argue. At the same time, inclusionism can be developed into a fruitful contextual approach when it comes to dealing with non-Western cultures and peoples attempting to transmit the message of Christ to them. However, as noted, the average Japanese may not be able to understand the Christian concept of "exclusive salvation" as it is presented to them by missionaries, for this claim of exclusivity causes disturbances in the overall *wa* (chapter three). Accepting Christianity as their only religion has many problematic consequences, as noted above.

We now return to the rhetorical question posed at the beginning of this chapter, namely "where does Christianity fit in Prince Shotoku's statement?" Christian missionaries offer salvation through one religion only. Ideally, this requires a total conversion, rejection of one's former religious ideas and culture and surrender to a new belief system. In and of itself, this concept of conversion runs contrary to the notion of inclusivity that is the primary hallmark of Japanese culture. For most Japanese, it is hard to "convert" to a new religion that promotes a total exclusive commitment to a religious system and so obviates against any adaptation to, or co-existence with, other existing traditions.

85

The *kakure Kirishitans* combined Buddhism and Christianity in a kind of syncretism with Shinto and Buddhism. As Christal Whelan writes:

> "The syncretism of Buddhist and Christian traditions in the *Tenchi* is notable and reminiscent, too, of the earlier commingling of Buddhism and Shinto known as *honji-suijaku*. Accordingly, the Buddhist deities were considered as fundamental or original *(honji)* and the Shinto deities *(kami)* as their manifestation *(suijaku)*. A similar sort of Buddhist–Christian co-existence is revealed in telling phrases like this one: "As for the one you worship as Buddha, he is called *Deusu*, Lord of Heaven. He is the Buddha who introduced the salvation to help humankind in the world yet to come.""[42]

In what follows, I describe the views of some Japanese theologians who believed that Christianity can be combined with Shinto, Buddhism and Confucianism as they existed in Japan when Christianity arrived. Further, I will discuss some rites and ceremonies and comment on the way in which Japanese Christians relate to them. Do converts to Christianity completely abandon these ceremonies, or do they find a way to combine them with their Christian faith?

Danjo Ebina (1866–1937) held that Christianity embodied universal truth and so plays a purifying role in human history. He insisted that, if Shinto were to become purified, it would turn into

Christianity. He also proposed that Confucianism and Christianity were actually compatible. Still, he more or less neglected the major differences between these religions.[43]

Hiromichi Kozaki (1856–1928) tried to build a bridge between Christianity and Confucianism. He argued that, even though Confucianism does not directly relate to Christianity, it does not contradict Christianity. He compares the function of Confucianism with Judaism. Like Judaism, it prepares the way for Christianity in Japan.[44] In his view, Christianity goes beyond Confucianism; it perfects and fulfills it. Confucian loyalty can be applied to the God of Christianity, and thus the meaning of belief and obedience to God becomes clear.[45] Uchimura also referred to the traditional Japanese faith and urged the Japanese Christians to recognize the considerable contribution that their own tradition had made to their belief in Christianity. Much of what seemed to Japanese to be unprecedented within Christianity was actually already present in their native beliefs.[46] He states,

> I am blamed by the missionaries for upholding Japanese Christianity. They say that Christianity is a universal religion, and to uphold Japanese Christianity is to make a universal religion a national religion. Very true! But do not these very missionaries uphold sectional or denominational forms of Christianity which are not very different from national Christianity? Is not Episcopalianism essentially an English Christianity, Presbyterianism a Scotch

Christianity, Lutheranism a German Christianity, and so forth? Why, for instance, call a universal religion 'Cumberland Presbyterianism?' If it is not wrong to apply the name of a district in the state of Kentucky to Christianity, why is it wrong to apply the name of my country to the same? I think I have as much right to call my Christianity Japanese as thousands of Christians in Cumberland Valley have the right to call their Christianity by the name of the valley they live in."[47]

And, he also proposed that:

In terms of nature of faith, we should join the (Buddhist priests) Genshin (942–1017), Honen and Shinran; in terms of evangelical means, we should learn from the Confucian scholar Ito Jinsai (1627–1705), Nakae Toju and Kaibara Ekken (1630–1714). Then without dependence on foreigners we should believe in Christ and spread His gospel.[48]

Kanzo Uchimura is not the only theologian who tried to use Japanese native religions as a platform for advancing Christianity in Japan. Katsumi Takizawa (1904–1984), and Seiichi Yagi are among many others who attempted this. For example, Yagi argues that initially Japanese theology needed Western theology as its protector. However, this long dependence has led to the development of bad habits such as Japanese Christians refusing to read any theological work written by native Japanese theologians. He observes that some Japanese are even ashamed of referring to Japanese studies in the bibliographies appended to the work of Japanese authors.[49] Thus, Yagi encouraged the development of Christianity in the Japanese context, and in the context of Japanese Buddhism in particular. He wrote various books on this topic, such as *Contact Points between Buddhism and Christianity* (1975) and *Paul/Shinran, Jesus/Zen* (1979).

Lastly, Sherrill made the following interesting point about salvation in Japan: salvation occurs precisely because one has experienced a healing that picks up the scattered fragments of a life and shapes them again into a single story, filling the void left by meaninglessness.[50] He notes,

> "Religious seekers in contemporary Japan are not so much looking for personal salvation as they are relational redemption. For this reason, religion as rational knowing—which is essentially how the church in Japan presents Christianity—has little chance of connecting with contemporary society. "On an individual level, we can identify a reaction against the separation of body and spirit in modern society and a protest against the attenuation of human relationships. On a wider social level, increased interest in environmental concerns has contributed to current interest in healing."[51]

4.3.2 The Infallibility of the Bible

Most Christian denominations, especially Evangelical missionaries, consider the Bible to be the infallible Word of God. The Japan Evangelical Missionary Association's (JEMA) first article in its statement of faith reads:

> "We believe in the Holy Scriptures as originally given by God, verbally inspired, infallible, entirely trustworthy; and the supreme authority in all matters of faith and conduct. (2 Tim. 3:16; 2 Peter 1:21)[52]

But the notion of the infallibility of the Bible also does not fit into the inclusivist, relativist Japanese cultural framework. The claim that one book alone is the Word of God, and that upon conversion to Christianity, one has to read it and to live by it absolutely may not be easily understood by most Japanese people. To them, reading the Bible does not mean denying the sacredness of other Japanese religious or spiritual works. Even among Japanese theologians there are different views about the Bible, let alone among the average Japanese who has little or no basic knowledge regarding the Bible. For instance, according to Hiromichi Kozaki (1856–1938), faith and reason are not in conflict with each other, but are interdependent. This results in the view that the Holy Spirit sanctifies reason. It moved him to suggest that the Bible was inspired by God, but that its words are not necessarily infallible. Kozaki believed that even the theory of evolution could be harmonized with the content of the Bible, and this viewpoint influenced his interpretation of the

Bible.[53]Such views are often criticized by Western missionaries and even by some Japanese theologians, such as Masahisa Uemura (1857–1925) whose theology was influenced by the evangelical theology of the West.[54]

Ebina considered the notion of Logos to be more important than the Bible itself. In his view, this Logos is present in nature and in the history and literature of Japan; it is also found every wherein the world.[55] This understanding of the Logos being present in the "nature, history and literature of the Japanese" can be adapted to the view of co-existence and harmony of religions in Japan. Ebina even suggests that when this Logos was actualized among the people of Japan, a new Bible or a scripture should emerge from them. He believed that the Logos or the living spirit of God cannot be limited to one book.[56] As he states,

> "Therefore, we must expect the emergence of something superior to the Bible. In reading of the Bible, I do not value the whole Bible equally. We have to select from the Scriptures what seems to be given by God to us today. We should fill the spirit in the world of literature to produce a new bible through the urge of the heavenly inspiration."[57]

4.4 Japanese Rituals and Christianity

Another point related to the view of "salvation through Christianity-only" is that of tolerance toward native religious rituals. Often, Western Christianity has not been tolerant of local, cultural practices.

But, as noted, rituals and ceremonies are essential in Japanese culture. Even when one is not religious *per se*, he or she values participation in ceremonies as a very important act. This serves primarily to maintain social harmony, and makes it possible not to lose face with others in the group.

David Reid conducted research on Japanese participation in religious culture. The results of his work are described in his book *New Wine: The Cultural Shaping of Japanese Christianity* (1991). His questionnaire was entitled *Nihonjin no shukyo bunka ni kansuru ishiki chosa* (A survey of Japanese people's attitudes toward religious culture). It was a multiple-choice questionnaire that was be returned anonymously.[58] In total, there were 451 respondents, of which 200 were non-Christian (Shinto, Buddhist, other, none) and 251 Christian.[59] Although this research may not be very recent, I take it to be relevant and so discuss some of its findings here, especially those which concern altars or traditional or religious rites or ceremonies.

Among the 251 Christian respondents, 25 percent confirmed that there was a Buddha altar *(butsudan)* in their homes.[60] Most Japanese homes contain two sacred altars, one attributed to Buddha *(butsudan)* and one to the native gods *(kamidana)*. It is worthwhile to again note the co-existence of these two religions here. Buddhism and Shinto each have their own place in Japanese homes. This goes back to the notion of harmony and the importance of maintaining it and co-existing with those who hold different beliefs and traditions.

Further, 19 percent of those who have *butsudan* at home responded that they followed Buddhism as their religion.[61] This may

92

seem quite confusing to an outsider, but it is understandable within the Japanese context. Reid argues that one is thinking stereotypically if one suggests that no "traditional" Christian Japanese home will have a *butsudan*. As noted, 25 percent confirmed that they do have one. However, to the Christian respondents who indicated that they did not have an altar in their home, it seemed improper and shameful that there were Christians who did. They expressed a wish that this finding not become public knowledge— especially that it not be made known to people in other countries. Reid explains that this attitude of shame is probably strongest among the Japanese Christians who associate having a *butsudan* at home with "ancestor worship".[62]

Concerning the presence of religious objects in the home, 65 percent of the Japanese Christian respondents who confirmed that they have *butsudan* also confirmed that they have a *kami* altar in their homes, 65 percent have a shrine talisman, 68 percent have Buddhist mortuary tablets, and 40 percent have Buddhist sutras, and 40 percent have memorial photos. Further, among those Christians that have a *butsudan*, 85 percent also do not have a cross or crucifix in their home, although 95 percent have a Bible.[63] When a child is born to a family, according to Reid's report, 23 percent of the Christian respondents visit a Shinto shrine with the baby; 26 percent visit a Shinto shrine or Buddhist temple at the New Year.[64]

A sense of connection with one's ancestors was also quite evident among the Christian respondents: approximately 56 percent of those who also have an altar at home, and 46 percent of those who do not, responded that there are times when they feel closely connected to their ancestors.[65] In this connection, 17 percent of the Christians who were questioned routinely make requests before a *butsudan*, and 25 percent of those responded that they even report significant matters (to the ancestors) when they are before the altar. Almost 60 percent of the Christian respondents requested that a Buddhist priest officiate at memorial services.[66]

Most of the Japanese people believe in the dual nature of humankind as well as in the immortality of the spirit. When a person dies, the spirit leaves the body and goes to another world while the flesh perishes. The ancestral spirit comes back to this world after completing a certain process. In other words, humans and gods co-exist, they reside within the same continuum; there is no clear-cut boundary between them like there is between God and humanity in Christianity.[67] A *shiryo*, the spirit of the deceased, gradually diminishes in its spiritual power and rises in rank from *shiryo* to *hotoke* and then to *kami* through the repetition of ancestral veneration rites practiced by the family members. The *kami* is the ancestral spirit that is "created" when close relatives sincerely carry out religious rites. These ancestral spirits live near their home location and return at *Obon* and New Year's Day. The Japanese believe that they bring abundant harvests and wellbeing to the people; they are also thought to reincarnate.[68]Also, the *kakure kirishitans* (hidden Christians during the persecution in the Tokugawa era and subsequently) continued to perform ancestral veneration as much as other Japanese.[69] Turnbull suggests that, "when Christians went underground the persistent belief in ancestor worship, hallowed by missionaries' apparent encouragement, provided the precise mechanism of memorialization that the secret believers needed. It also provided a means of expression that was perfect camouflage for secret Christian beliefs."[70] However, according to Kentaro Miyazaki, this ancestral veneration by the *kakure* makes them no longer to consider Jesus Christ or the Holy Trinity as their only God; "it is now the souls of ancestors, particularly those who chose gruesome deaths over renunciation of Christianity. The *kakure kirishitan* therefore consider it their foremost duty—and the highest expression of their faith—to loyally maintain the religious system for which their ancestors gave up their lives."[71]

As noted in previous chapters, the Japanese view life in relational terms with others. In other words, these "others" are not only living humans, but also ancestors. So, what do all the data presented here suggest? They indicate that even though there are those who confess Christianity, still at least a subgroup of them continue to follow Christianity without abandoning their native cultural and religious traditions.

4.5 The Japanese After-Life and Christianity

What happens after a person dies? What do the relatives do and what do they believe happens to the deceased person? A series of rites and rituals takes place, the aim of which is to remove the dead soul from this world and install it as an ancestral spirit by enshrining it in the home of its living family. It is believed that the spirit of the deceased person will move around the house for 49 days.[72] Within this time period various kinds of rites are conducted and Buddhist priests recite various prayers. Through these prayers and rituals, the essence of Buddhism will be symbolically transmitted to the spirit and the spirit will thus be cleansed of all the pollutions associate with death. The soul is thereby prepared to be enshrined at the *butsudan* as an ancestral spirit.[73] On the seventh day after a person has passed away, he or she is be given a posthumous name, *kaimyo,* conferred by the priest from the family temple. Through the priest's reading of the Buddhist scriptures and through the "being listened to," the spirit of the deceased person is believed to become enlightened. The new name given to that person and his enlightened identity are a new stage in the purification process.[74] Eventually the *kaimyo* will be inscribed on a memorial tablet, *ihai,* which is placed on the *butsudan*. At first, two temporary *ihai* are made; one is placed at the grave and one at the *butsudan*. Forty-nine days after the death of the individual, and after all the necessary rites have been conducted, the spirit leaves the environs of the family and enters the ancestral world. At this time the permanent *ihai* of lacquer embossed in gold with the *kaimyo* is engraved on it and it is placed on the *butsudan*.[75] Many believe that the spirit of the ancestor will now abide in the *ihai*. Thus, the ancestors are present in the home in the form of enlightened souls; they are spirits who reside with the family. It is also interesting to note that during physical emergencies or calamities, the *ihai* are rescued first—this fact underscores the importance of the ancestors in Japanese culture.

Inevitably, the Japanese views on ancestors and the spirits of the dead are at odds with Christian doctrine and practices as espoused by evangelicals or Pentecostals. Rituals for the dead, making tablets, and believing the spirit will be liberated or enlightened through prayers are not considered acceptable in Christianity. In some Christian circles, they are even considered sinful. It is clear that the Japanese cannot therefore not easily come to understand how Christianity deals with ancestors and how it views life after death. However, there are some notable attempts by the Japanese theologians to offer alternatives, or to propose that an indigenous approach be taken in dealing with the dead and with the issue of life after death. In the following paragraph, I discuss one of the common theological/religious questions that most Japanese ask when they are evangelized: "What about our ancestors? Did they go to the Christian hell?" This reminds me of the story Brinkman discussed in his book, *The Non-Western Jesus* (2009): the eight-century Frisian King Radboud who was about to be baptized by the priest, asked before his baptism about the fate of his non-baptized ancestors; he decided not to be baptized, after the priest replied that they were in hell.[76]

Just like King Radboud, the Japanese people are very much concerned with the condition of their ancestors, as well as with their deceased relatives. But such concerns are also prevalent among Japanese Christians. According to Brinkman a number of Japanese churches are familiar with substitutionary baptism in connection with the practice of *mizuko kuyo*[77]. As the abortion rate is high in Japan, a lot of women feel guilty about their abortion and fear that the wandering spirit of their children may curse them and even take revenge. Thus, if someone else can be baptized for these unborn children and the forgiveness of sins is proclaimed in that baptism, all these children can be led, through Christ, from the kingdom of death to the kingdom of heaven.[78] Also, some Christians in Japan practice substitution celebration of Communion and this is considered to be a help to the dead. In this service, the descendants receive bread and wine on behalf of the deceased, believing that the deceased have received these gifts in heaven in a spiritual way.[79]

Some Japanese Christians have developed and discussed the possibility of indigenous alternatives to Christian teaching that include ancestors within the message of the Gospel, and do this without losing their reverence for them. In the following paragraphs I discuss one of these alternatives.

4.5.1 Second Chance Theory

In 2002, Tsugumichi Okawa, a pastor of a large church in Tokyo, announced at a Sunday service that was broadcast live on television, that he believed in the Second Chance Theory. Sekundo Chansu Ron (セカンドチャンス論) or Second Chance Theory is an ongoing discussion point in Japanese Christianity. It affirms that those who have never heard the gospel do not go directly to hell, but instead go to Hades, which is not the same thing. At the end of time, they will have a second chance to hear the gospel and make a choice to believe in Christ. Okawa also openly declared that Hades is not hell, that the two are different, and that everyone who dies without hearing the gospel in their lifetime will hear it in Hades. However, this caused a major controversy among Christians in Japan. The July 2002 issue of *Hazah Magazine* carried a six-month long debate between affirmationists and denialists on this question. Even though this theory did not originate in Japan, it may fit within the Japanese context of ancestral veneration.

The Second Chance Theory was first articulated by a Scottish theologian named William Barclay (1907–1978), a New Testament scholar and an advocate of Second Chance Theology. Yoshinobu Kumazawa, ex-president of Tokyo Union Theological Seminary, and Tsuneaki Kato, professor at the same seminary, although they did explicitly use the term Second Chance, they preached something similar to this. Kumazawa taught that Jesus descended to Hades and preached his Good News to the people there."[80] In a sermon delivered at denominational conference of the United Church of Christ in Tokyo he said:

> "There often arises the question what would happen to those who died without faith, especially to my close people. People sometimes can't decide to be baptized, thinking, 'If my beloved family would not be saved, how could only I be baptized?' What does the Bible say about that? . . . I can refer to the following verses. I Peter 3:19 . . . There it is written that Christ descended to the world of the dead, that is Hades (Sheol) . . . Hades is different from Gehenna, or hell. It is written that Christ went down to the world of the dead, to the people who died without believing in Christ, and Christ preached his gospel to them. Apostle Peter tells us that this was for the grace of Christ to be spread over the people who died without knowing Christ"[81]

Arimasa Kubo, in his article, "Salvation For the Dead: Second Chance Theology," writes extensively on the validity of such theology. He says:

> In addition, denying the second chance for the dead people in Hades has ever presented major difficulties to evangelism, especially in the East, for a vast majority of ancestors of Oriental civilizations never had the chance to hear the Gospel of Christ. People of Eastern cultures revere their ancestors very much. One Japanese person who chose against becoming a Christian writes: "I asked a Christian missionary, 'Where are my ancestors?' He answered, 'In Hell.'" So I asked again, 'Is there any way to save them from there?' He replied, 'No way.' When I heard it, I decided not to become a Christian. Western person is generally individualistic, and he may be able to become a Christian even knowing that his ancestors are in hell. But I don't want to go to Heaven alone when all of my ancestors are in hell with no hope. I don't want to believe in God who does such an unreasonable thing." Everyone in the East understands this sentiment. Denying the second chance in Hades has ever kept people from knowing Christ. Furthermore, this denial is based on the confusion of Hades with hell, a prime heresy of Bible interpretations.[82]

In his book, *The Biblical Theory of the Second Chance (Seisho-teki sekandochansu-ron, 2006)*, Arimasa Kubo elaborates this theory and confirms that it is biblically supported and can be used for purposes of evangelism.

However, the idea of Second Chance is not limited to Japan. According to Brinkman, this idea of "descended into hell" was widespread in the Christianity of the East and West for centuries. He even indicates that we still find in the Apostle's Creed that later erratic addition which concerns the decent to hell.[83] Brinkman indicates that, according to the testimony of the Rufinius (end of the fourth century), the idea that Jesus "descended into hell" appeared in the baptismal confessions of Aquileia and the synods of Sirmium (357) and Nice (359). They were already familiar with the idea that Christ descended into hell, (1 Peter 4:6), that the even dead had to be told the Good News as well.[84] These dead were considered to be in a "waiting room" for both the just and unjust who were separated when Christ died and descended to hell.[85] Brinkman concludes that a complicated text such as 1 Peter 3:19 appears to mean that those who die as unbelievers are given another opportunity for conversion after Christ's redemption.[86] According to Brinkman this concept of being "descended to hell" can be more easily linked with the importance that is attached to ancestors by non-Western peoples of Africa and Asia.[87]

From the brief discussion in this chapter, one can conclude that there are various theological themes that are subjects of disagreement and discussion among Japanese theologians, and also among Japanese people and Christian missionaries (or fellow

Japanese Christians) who are evangelizing them. In the following chapter, I therefore discuss possible missiological factors related to the low acceptance rate of Christianity in Japan.

Notes

1 Davies and Ikeno, 128.

2 Ichiro Hori, *Folk Religion in Japan: Continuity and Change* (Chicago: University of Chicago Press, 1968), 10.

3 There are ongoing debates whether Confucianism is a religion or a philosophy. For the sake of clarity I consider Confucianism as a religion as it was mentioned in the list of religions in Prince Shotoku's statement.

4 Psalm 51:5, Psalm 58:3, Romans 3:2.

5 1Corinthians 15:22.

6 Romans 8:19.

7 Gary Leazer, "Shintoism," *Center for Interface Studies' Bulletin,* (2010), 3.

8 Paul de Leeuw, "Naka-Ima: Space in Japan," *The Netherlands-Japan Review,* Volume 2, nr.1, Spring (2011): 46-47.

9 "Statement of Faith," Japan Evangelical Missionary Association, accessed April 17, 2013, http://www.jema.org/joomla15/index.php/jema-constitution-and-bylaws/415-jema-constitution?start=2.

10 J. Nelson Jennings, *Theology in Japan: Takakura Tokutaro, 1885–1934* (Lanham: University Press of America, 2005), 244.

11 Ibid.

12 Yoji Inoue, *The Faces of Jesus in Japan* (Tokyo: Nihon Kirisuto-Kyodan Shuppankyi, 1994), 36.

13 Ibid.

14 Ibid.

15 Moriyuki Abukuma (ed.), *Daily Devotions with Uchimura Kanzo* (Amsterdam: Foundation Press, 2010), 5.

16 Carlo Caldarola, *Christianity: The Japanese Way* (Leiden: Brill, 1979), 12–13.

17 Bernard S. Silberman, (ed.), *Japanese Character and Culture: A Book of Selected Readings* (Tucson: University of Arizona Press, 1962), 299.

18 Sansom, 51.

19 Ibid.

20 Ibid.

21 Matthew 15:11, NIV.

22 Makito Nagasawa, "Makuya Pentecostalism: A Survey" in *Asian Journal of Pentecostal Studies* 3/2 (2000), 213.

23 David Lewis, "Questioning Assumptions About Japanese Society" Hayama Missionary Seminar Report 1988, PDF Version 1.1, November 2008, 19.

24 Ibid.

25   Lewis, 20.

26   Lewis, 17-18.

27   Lewis, 18.

28   Shusaku Endo, *Silence* (New Jersey: Taplinger Publishing Company, 1980), 89.

29   Hasegawa, 68.

30   Hasegawa, 69.

31   Ibid.

32   Caldarola, 112.

33   Inagaki and Jennings, 38.

34   Inagaki and Jennings, 39.

35   Martien E. Brinkman, *The Non-Western Jesus: Jesus as Bodhisattva, Avatara, Guru, Prophet, Ancestor or Healer?* (London: Equinox Publishing Ltd., 2009), 102.

36   John F. Howes, *Japan's Modern Prophet: Uchimura Kanzo 1861– 1930* (Vancouver: University of British Columbia, 2005), 231.

37   Acts 4:12. John 14:6.

38   Hendry, 139.

39   Ibid.

40   Mullins 1998, 61. Mullins refers here to *The Complete Works of Uchimura Kanzo* vol.29, (1925-1926), 456.

41 Inagaki and Jennings, 90-91. Inagaki and Jennings quote here
from Katsumi Takizawa 's *Kami wa ooku no namae o motsu*
(God Has Many Names), (Tokyo: Iwanami Shoten, 1986), 117.

42 Whelan, 28.

43 Yasuo Furuya (ed.), *A History of Japanese Theology*
(Grand Rapids: Wm. B. Eerdmans Publishing Co., 1997), 13.

44 Furuya, 15.

45 Furuya, 15-16.

46 Howes, 232.

47 Mullins 1998, 37. Mullins refers to *"Complete Work
of Uchimura Kanzo"* vol.29, (1925–1926) 476–47.

48 Howes, 232.

49 Furuya, 6.

50 Sherrill, 177.

51 Sherrill, 176. Sherrill refers to Tatsuya Yumiyama, "Varieties of
Healing in Present-Day Japan." *Japanese Journal of Religious
Studies* 22/3-4 (1995), 267-82.

52 "Statement of Faith," Japan Evangelical Missionary Association,
accessed April 17, 2013, http://www.jema.org/joomla15/index.
php/jema-constitution-and-bylaws/415-jema-constitution?start=2.

53 Furuya, 31.

54 Furuya, 49.

55 Yumi Murayama-Cain, "The Bible in the Imperial Japan 1850 –
1950"(PhD diss., University of St. Andrews, 2010), 70.

56 Ibid.

57 Murayama-Cain, 70. Murayama-Cain refers here to Ebina's
"Sachiwau Kotodama" (Blessed Logos) in Shinjin 7, no. 12
(1906), 6.

58 David Reid, *New Wine: The Cultural Shaping of Japanese
Christianity* (Berkeley: Asian Humanities Press, 1991), 123.

59 Reid, 124.

60 Reid, 125.

61 Reid, 126.

62 Reid, 130-131. (There are ongoing discussions on whether
ancestor worship and veneration of ancestors are the same or
not. In the eyes of the general Christian public they may be the
same, but not among intellectual theological groups. Generally, in
Christianity one does not worship ancestors; in my opinion, it may
be a taboo to even venerate one's ancestors. Thus, having a
butsudan makes some Japanese Christians uncomfortable because
their brothers and sisters from other parts of the world, especially
from the West, may learn that some Japanese Christians still have
butsudans in their homes.)

63 Reid, 133.

64 Reid, 143.

65 Reid, 137.

66 Reid, 138.

67 Fukuda, 58.

68 Fukuda, 62–3.

69 Stephen Turnbull, *The Kakure Kirishitan of Japan: A Study of their
Development, Beliefs and Rituals to the Present Day* (Richmond:
Japan Library, 1988), 199.

70 Ibid.

71 Miyazaki Kentaro, "Hidden Christians in Contemporary Nagasaki"
in Crossroads the Online Journal of Nagasaki History and culture
http://www.uwosh.edu/home_pages/faculty_staff/earns/
miyazaki.html

72 Reader, 90.

73 Ibid.

74 Ibid.

75 Reader, 91.

76 Brinkman, 124.

77 *Mizuko*, literally means "water child". This is a Japanese term
for a dead fetus or, archaically, a dead baby or infant. Mizuko kuyo
or "fetus memorial service," is a Japanese ceremony for those
who have had a miscarriage, stillbirth, or abortion.

78 Brinkman, 126.

79 Brinkman, 124.

80 wikipedia.org/wiki/セカンドチャンス_(キリスト教)

81   Speech delivered by Yoshikata Kumano at the Denominational
     Conference at United Church of Christ in Tokyo, during Aug.
     19-20, 1972.

82   Arimasa Kubo, "Salvation for the Dead, Second Chance Theology:
     Hades is Not Hell" http://www2.biglobe.ne.jp/~remnant/
     hades.htm

83   Martien E. Brinkman, *The Tragedy of Human Freedom: The Failure
     and Promise of the Christian Concept of Freedom in Western Culture*
     (Amsterdam: Rodopi B.V., 2003), 91.

84   Ibid.

85   Brinkman 2003, 89.

86   Brinkman 2003, 92.

87   Ibid.

Chapter 5

MISSIOLOGICAL FACTORS

This chapter is divided into three major parts: the first two are brief descriptions of Christian mission, both Catholic and Protestant. I describe missionaries' strategies, struggles as well as their influence on Japanese society. In the third part, I discuss some conclusions that can perhaps be drawn regarding missionary work in Japan, both in the past and the present. Here I consider three possible errors committed by Western missionaries in the past; these are related to their: (1) a Eurocentric approach; (2) a lack of consideration for cultural context; and (3) denominational competitiveness. These errors are also discussed in this chapter.

5.1 Roman Catholic Missionaries

During the first 30 years of the Jesuit mission to Japan (1549–1585), only a limited amount of Christian doctrinal information was passed on to the Japanese people. This was due to the linguistic barrier, and also to the small number of mission personnel available to convey the teachings. Non-verbal means are assumed to have been used (for example, Christian symbols and rituals).[1] In this same period, the Jesuits missionaries opted to rely on a strategy of adaptation. They had no choice but to try to conform to Japanese customs and religious manners, to become a part of Japanese society and to function within the Japanese system of life. Succinctly stated, foreign missionaries had a serious communication problem with the Japanese. For both parties, language was an enormous barrier. The missionaries did not know how to express themselves in Japanese, nor did they know how to translate Christian terminology into Japanese; conversely, the Japanese were unable to speak either Spanish or Portuguese.

The key figure responsible for translation from Portuguese to Japanese was Anjiro (Paul).[2] Anjiro viewed Christian theological concepts from the perspective of a Buddhist layman. When he wrestled with Christian concepts and their theological meanings in order to translate them into Japanese, he almost had no choice except to use various Buddhist terminologies. Ebisawa Arimichi suggests that these were perhaps the only means available for expressing the salvific religious and philosophical concepts of Christianity.[3]

As the early missionaries progressed in their knowledge of the Japanese language, they realized that the word *dainichi* was not suitable for the Christian God. From then on, they called God Deus *(Deusu)* or *hotoke*, which is a more generic term for Buddha.[4] Xavier therefore changed the translation for the word "God" from *dainichi* to Deus (pronounced *deusu* by the Japanese). So, from that point, it was preached in the streets of Yamaguchi that *dainichi* was not the true God and should not be prayed to. Gradually, this created enmity between Buddhist monks and the missionaries. The Buddhist saw the missionaries as rivals and competitors.[5] This pronunciation of *Deusu* was also not considered appropriate for the Japanese because *Deusu* is close to *Daiuso*, which means "big mouth"[6] or the English equivalent, a "big lie." Thereafter, all other borrowed

Japanese terms were also directly retranslated into their Latin and Portuguese equivalents. Anjiro's name subsequently disappeared from the Jesuits' writings.

During this first 30 years of the Catholic mission, the main part of the Christian message was transmitted via Christian symbols and rituals. The Japanese converts therefore engaged with their new religion through symbols, rituals and relics. Since the Japanese religious culture was already based on rituals and symbols, it made it easier for converts to adapt to the new Christian (i.e., Roman Catholic) rituals. As Higashibaba states:

> The overall symbolic system, viz., religious system of the Japanese followers remained intact even after they began to use Christian symbols. For the system to be intact, symbolic constituents integrated within the system had to keep functioning in their proper positions, for the same purpose. People's engagement with Christian symbols can be understood as either substituting new symbols for existing symbols or adding new symbols to old ones. In either case the motivation on the part of the followers is the mysterious power which they found in the new symbols. When they found these so powerful that they no longer needed the old ones, they adopted new and discarded the old. When the new symbols were thought to be less powerful but useful, however, they used them as a backup for the older ones.[7]

111

These symbols and rituals underwent two major phases of adaptation during this period: 1) The introduction of new symbols or rituals to the Japanese religious context, and 2) the replacement of old rituals with a combination of the newly introduced rituals and old rituals. Eventually both came to be used simultaneously. Such adaptation did not always reflect the essence of the Christian message, instead it led to a form of syncretism.

The missionaries gradually left Japan due to the negative sentiments directed against them and Christianity went underground. It was during and after the Meiji Period that Catholic missionaries re-entered the country. They were more or less engaged in directing the *kakure Kirishitan* back to Roman Catholicism. Even though they settled in major cities, they focused their efforts on rural areas. However, they experienced more opposition there than the Protestants who were active in the urban areas.

5.2 Protestant Missionaries

In the early Meiji Period, Protestantism was organizationally transmitted to Japan through two channels: mission boards and church agencies. The missionaries who set foot on Japanese soil in 1858 were sponsored by one of these two "channels". Protestants were, in fact, invited or offered employment by Japanese organizations, such as schools.

Reverend G.F. Verbeck (1830–1898), one of the first of these missionaries, was employed by the Japanese government for a considerable time. Several other persons, who arrived in the country as government-employed instructors, exerted a profound and positive influence on its Protestant history. A number of young Japanese became Christian in Yokohama, Kumamoto, and Sapporo through the influence of Protestant missionaries. They were mainly of the samurai class and so from clans that had supported the now defunct shogunate. Socially, they were viewed as losers. Still, they were well educated in Confucian ethics as an elite class, and were motivated to undertake advanced foreign studies, which were available only through missionaries. Although they generally intended to form denominational churches in keeping with their backgrounds, these missionaries had to cooperate with each other since Christianity was still very much a minority in Japan. In spite of this, there were a few who intentionally pursued non-denominational evangelism.

Those who came as missionaries during this period were generally of the puritan and evangelical faith. They were therefore from the tradition of revivalism: Pietism, the Great Awakening, and the Methodist movement. This bridged the denominational gap.[8] In the 1880s, Japanese churches experienced a revival, one which united Christians in that country. Initially, missionaries did not pay much attention to academic theology,[9] but at this time the church grew with such speed that many Christians believed that Japan would soon become a Christian nation. According to Fujiwara, this growth depended largely upon Japanese acceptance of Western culture. When Japan later turned toward nationalism, the church had to struggle.[10]

Between 1883 and 1889, the word "revival" or *rebaibaru* was introduced into the Japanese language. This was one outcome

113

of the Osaka Missionary Conference in 1883. In that city, all the
denominations held four-week prayer meetings, the aim of which
was to pray especially for "the outpouring of the Holy Spirit." These
meetings resulted in a revival of interest in Christianity, one that
spread throughout the country. The outpouring of the Holy Spirit
was also felt in the great social meeting of Japanese Christians
in May 1883. At Doshisha University in 1884, the classes spent
hours together in tears, prayers, and praise. The Sendai revival of
1886 and the Oita revival of 1888 are worthy of special mention
on account of the unusual events that occurred and the wonderful
experiences they produced. It was because of them that people
began to show more and more interest in Bible studies.[11]

Between 1887 and 1907, State Shinto became established
in Japan. During this period, nationalism grew stronger than
Westernism and Japan established an Emperor-centered institutional
system supported by State Shinto. Some scholars believe that
State Shinto was established with the deification of the Emperor
as one of its central doctrines and that this itself was a reaction
to the growing presence of Western Christianity in the country. In
other words, Shinto seems to have been institutionalized in an effort
to halt the ongoing process of Christianization.[12] Fujiwara suggests
that Western Christianity was a threat to Japan. He argues that this
was the case particularly because of Japan's nationalistic spiritual
pride, an attitude that is related to its inferiority complex vis-à-vis
Western technology.[13] It was, however, also partially due to the
nature of Western Christianity, namely to the fact that it provided a
spiritual motivation for imperialism. Thus, one can safely generalize

114

that Japan established the entity of State Shinto in response to a perceived threat from triumphal Western Christianity.[14]

From 1907 to 1926, the Japanese government had a relatively positive attitude toward missionaries. Christian schools and churches were established and the government looked for dialogue between Christianity and State Shinto with the aim of asking Christians to respect, and even serve under, the nation's State Shinto. In the early 1930s, State Shinto became considerably stronger and more severe. The government urged Christians to unite, but under the institution of Shinto. Thus, the *Nihon Kirisuto Kyodan* or "the United Church of Christian Japan" was formed next year, and its representative went to the *Ise* shrine to report this to *Amaterasu Oomikami,* the Sun goddess of Japan.[15] The *Kyodan* declared that Japanese Christians were Japanese subjects, and that they wished to pledge their loyalty to Japan by taking part in leading the spirit of the people beyond the denominational walls created by Christianity and by assisting the Imperial rule.[16]

During this period, missionaries had a very difficult time in Japan and they left the country after the war commenced in 1941. When the Pacific War ended and the Occupation of Japan by the Allied Forces began in 1945, Shintoism was abolished as the national religion, worship of the Emperor became prohibited, and missionaries resumed their activities. The post-war constitution guaranteed freedom of religion and separation of church and state. Still, Christians in Japan faced difficulties in their effort to re-introduce Christianity during the rebuilding process. However, substantial cooperation between missionaries and church leaders fostered the

115

recovery of the Japanese church. At the same time, their combined relief work encouraged many non-Christian Japanese to see Christianity in a positive light, as a pacifistic and liberal influence on the nation.[17] According to Sherrill, as the church sought to address the physical needs of the people, many Japanese discovered spiritual fulfillment in the Christian community. The post-World War II missionaries dedicated themselves to the evangelization of the nation, but they did a good deal of charity and relief work. They also offered foreign language classes in an attempt to reach out to and evangelize the Japanese.[18]

5.3 The Eurocentric Approach

Western missionaries to Japan and other parts of the world took with them a certain amount of cultural baggage, namely a sense of cultural superiority and an ethnocentric worldview. The latter is often understood to be a hallmark of Western civilization— it was especially pronounced during the era of colonization. This ethnocentrism led to the development of the attitude that, even though the missionaries were guests in Japan, they did not fully respect the people or the country that was hosting them. In the past, they had come to evangelize the Japanese, but they had they also attempted to systematically strip away their cultural heritage instead of trying to find a proper place for Christianity within the Japanese cultural framework. As Joseph Kitagawa explains, more often than not, European and American missionaries attempted to westernize as well as Christianize the Japanese people and culture. Japanese converts were made to feel, consciously or unconsciously, that to

116

decide for Christ also implied the total surrender of their souls to the missionaries.[19] According to Robert Lee, the legacy of the modern (Protestant) missionaries to the Japanese church since the of the Meiji Restoration has been based in an Eurocentric understanding of history and civilization, and so part of the extension of Western culture throughout the world.[20]

During the Tokugawa Period, newly converted Christians systematically destroyed Shinto and Buddhist temples in keeping with the teachings of the missionaries. Some missionaries were even accused of cheating farmers in order to sell them off as slaves.[21] Hideyoshi criticized the destruction of Shinto and Buddhist temples by zealous Christian converts and the forced conversion of their vassals to the Roman Catholic faith. Takayama Ukon was one of the Christian warlords who participated in the destruction of Shinto and Buddhist temples.[22] Hideyoshi sent couriers to the Jesuit leader Coelho asking him several questions, including "why do they destroy Shinto and Buddhist temples and persecute bonzes (monks), instead of compromising with them?" He also asked why the Portuguese buy Japanese people and export them from their native land as slaves.[23] Coelho replied to Hideyoshi that the only reason why they were in Japan was to save souls and convert people to Christianity, and that they used only peaceful means. Concerning the slaves, he explained basically that they could not do anything about it since it was on Japanese soil and the Japanese natives sold them to the Portuguese traders.[24]

The Portuguese exchanged Japanese slaves for firearms and other Western products. In his reply to Hideyoshi's questions,

117

Coelho mentioned that the destruction of the temples was not done by the padres, but by the local Christians who had been inspired to do it. This, however, is not completely true. One Jesuit padre wrote the following:

> "God gave such a strength to the padres that they destroyed and burned all monasteries and temples of the bonzes, so that our law and the padres now acquired greater power and prestige than they had done previously"[25]

Another Catholic source writes, for instance, that outside the capital lay the mountain of Hieizan, also known as a stronghold of bonzes. At one point, there were more than 3,000 Buddhist monasteries in the area. Yet, over the period, this number was reduced to 600.[26] Concerning the destruction of the Shinto and Buddhist temples by the native Christians, one must ask why the missionaries could not have made an effort to teach them to respect—and so prohibit them from destroying—Shinto and Buddhist temples? The native Christians were disciples of these missionaries.

Coelho's reply to the question of slavery is evidence of the same pattern of thought: he blamed natives for trading in slaves instead of the Portuguese themselves who were, in fact, supported by Coelho's Jesuit missionaries. His response did not ease the situation and on July 25, 1587, Hideyoshi, ordered the Jesuit padres to leave Japan and return to their home country.

Missionaries considered native festivals and religious rites paganistic and unchristian. Thus, after their conversion, the Japanese people, especially the warlords, refused to participate in centuries-old Japanese religious festivals and ceremonies, including the ancestral adorations. Such attitudes, taken together with the destruction of temples and holy objects of the host nation, were intolerable to the natives—as they are to people from almost any culture. To the Japanese, in particular, such an attitude seemed arrogant and lacking proper respect. *Fukan Fabian* or *Fukunsai Habian* (1565–1621) is a very good example of a native Japanese seminarian, an intellectual who was trained by the Jesuits, but later turned against them.

According to Kiri Paramore "Fabian was a prominent Jesuit apologist, public speaker, and author of the famous Japanese Jesuit text *Myotei Mondo* (1605).[27] Through these activities he came to be identified as the most influential of all Japanese Christian thinkers of the so-called first period of Christianity in the Japan of the late sixteenth/early seventeenth centuries."[28] He was known as a charismatic orator and representative of the Jesuits in debates against notable Buddhist and Confucian figures.[29] However, after almost two decades of working with the Society of Jesus, he left the *Kirishitan* faith and became an intellectual debater and critic of the very faith that he had once advocated.

It is believed that one reason why he abandoned his *Kirishitan* belief was the discriminatory behavior of the Jesuits. His enormous commitment to the Society notwithstanding, he was never ordained a priest.[30] Fukan wrote:

Pride is the root of all evil and humility the foundation
of all good; so make humility your actions' base— is
what they urge upon people. And yet the Devil himself
could not measure up to them in arrogance! Could it
be their inborn national character? And because of
this arrogance they sink to brawls and quarrels with
the *bateren* (priests) of other factions in contentions
for influence, outdoing laymen in their wrangles. It's
quite a sad thing to see, worse even than one could
imagine—you can be sure of that![31]

On the other hand, Schrimpf suggests that Fukan's anti-Christian
ideas in *Ha Deusu* are the result of the anti-Christian edict of 1614.
This document stated that Japan rested on the unity of the three
teachings, Buddhism, Shintoism, and Confucianism and blamed
Christians for attacking these religions and trying to disturb and
undermine Imperial law. According to Schrimpf, Fukan demonstrates
his awareness of a "cultural" — or national — identity that defines
his judgment on religions. Because he is Japanese, he propagates
worship of the Buddha and *kami* and the maintenance of Confucian
morality.[32]

During and after the Meiji Period up until the end of World
War II, missionary work was, once again, more or less Eurocentric.
Also during this period and beyond, Christianity was closely identified
with Western civilization and with the Western powers.[33] According
to Ballhatchet, this was an advantage when attitudes to the West
were positive, but a drawback when the opposite was the case. As a

120

source of Western learning, Christianity had a definite appeal in the early years, particularly to ex-samurai from political domains that had been on the losing side in the Meiji Restoration; it also appealed to those for whom contacts with the West presented new opportunities in education, commerce and even politics. This included both the ex-samurai, and merchants or producers who either had developed, or wanted to develop, links with the treaty ports.[34]

During and after the Meiji Period, Roman Catholicism, Protestantism, and Orthodox churches sent missionaries to Japan. The majority of the incoming Protestant missionaries were American, with some contingents from Britain and Canada. Most were from mainstream denominations: Presbyterian and Reformed, Congregational, Methodist, Episcopal, and Baptist.[35] During the early Meiji Period, whereas Protestants strived to improve social conditions, the Catholic emphasis was on saving individual souls, working among the poverty-stricken and baptizing them. The Catholic Church also attempted to recover the *kakure Kirishitans*. Protestant missionaries mostly attracted intellectuals, such as ex-samurai and their children. Thus, when their converts and the "baby" Christians from educated backgrounds began to mature, there was a growing awareness of the clash between foreign missionaries and Japanese Christians. Kanzo Uchimura is a good example of this. The son of a former Samurai, he converted to Christianity through the influence of an American missionary in 1877. He argued that it was not actually the West that invented Christianity, but rather that the opposite was true; Christianity entered the West and made it the West of today. He believed that the West was ignorant of this and he held that

121

Westerners propagate Christianity as if it were their own religion; similarly, Asians rejects Christianity as if it were a Westerner's religion. He considered all those who did not consider Christianity an occidental religion to be foolish.[36]

Uchimura also claimed that the Christianity taught by foreigners, especially Americans, could not possibly save Japan. For him, American Christianity was too materialistic and worldly.[37] He argued that the whole world, especially the religious East, felt that they did not need to be taught by Americans when it came to religious matters.[38] He also believed that no program of missionary work could move an entire nation to embrace Christianity, although it might produce some converts. He believed that missionaries had destroyed other countries in many cases, such as Montezuma's empire in Mexico and the Peruvian Incan empire and argued that Christendom's work has always been aimed at absorption, destruction, and, in some cases, even annihilation of other cultures. He asked what assurances there were against missionaries killing people in China, Korea, and even Japan, when they had the chance.[39]

Kishida suggests that perhaps the American tendency toward self-centeredness causes most Americans to think that their culture is entirely legitimate, even superior, and, at the same time, to hold that the Japanese culture and others are inferior, lacking certain important elements.[40] The Americans tried to make the Japanese become like them; they wanted to turn Japan into a Christian country. Since they believed this was possible, they poured a great deal of money and effort into it.[41]

This Eurocentric view of the world, as it was represented by the missionaries to Japan, made Western Christianity unbearable to many Japanese people. Kaiseki Matsumura (1859–1939), an early convert of the Dutch Reformed missionary James Ballagh and a member of the Yokohama Band, illustrates the tensions that existed between missionary teachers and their students. Matsumura, who had returned to Ballagh's school to assist with the teaching and supervision of the students, recalls that on one occasion he explained to Ballagh that all their missionary work would be of no avail if they continued to treat the Japanese as no more than cooks or helper boys. In response, Mr. Ballagh's wife accused Matsumura of being possessed by the Devil because of the things he had said.[42] He was dismissed from his position at the school and isolated from the missionaries. Soon Matsumura started his own independent denomination called *The Way!*

After World War II, MacArthur encouraged American missionaries to go to Japan. In response, churches and mission agencies sent more than 5,000 missionaries there. In his view, the country needed Jesus. In the late 1940s and throughout the 1950s, MacArthur spoke freely about the idea that post-World War II Japan was going through a spiritual vacuum. He argued that all of its gods had failed—both its ostensibly invincible military and its supposedly divine Emperor. Now this conquered people had nothing. In 1955, MacArthur told US News and World Report, "no phase of the occupation has left me with a greater sense of personal satisfaction than my spiritual stewardship. The land was flooded with millions of Bibles and thousands of missionaries."[43] (See chapter seven)

The occupying army prohibited freedom of the press and broadcasting in Japan until 1952. Any book, publication, or broadcast that criticized the United States was forbidden. On the other hand, the Americans broadcast their propaganda to the Japanese public, based on their "War Guilt Information Program." The U.S. occupational authorities organized this program to implant war guilt in the minds of Japanese through "education."[44] According Eto, the occupiers during the "War Guilt Information Program" made sure that American ideas will be passed on to next generation by educational means, even in the twenty-first century.[45] According Kato, Eto was one of the first to study the role of censorship in the history of education in Japan, and has done the most extensive study. *Contained Realm of Discourse: Censorship Operation by the Occupational Forces and Postwar* Japan is written from a point of view that the American occupation itself was a "tragic encounter" between the United States and Japan.[46]

5.4 Lack of Consideration for Cultural Context

Miyake takes this demonstrated lack of consideration for cultural context to be a crucial weakness in the strategies of the Protestant missionaries. He speaks of a tendency among Japanese Christians (especially the evangelical and Pentecostal/Charismatic denominations) to regard Japanese culture as simple idolatry and Western culture as "Christian" and thus superior. This seems to be the general direction of the influence of missionary teaching.[47] Also, as Hiebert notes, the importation of its own cultural practices has made Christianity a foreign religion in many lands— it has alienated

Christian converts from their own peoples and cultures. It is this foreignness and not offense to the gospel itself that has often kept people from following Christ.[48]

During the Tokugawa Period, missionaries struggled to translate Christian terminology into Japanese. For example, as mentioned earlier, initially the word *dainichi* (a word borrowed from Buddhism) was used to address God and so to conceptualize Christian principles. Many Japanese welcomed Christianity because they took it to be part of Buddhism.[49] Xavier quickly understood he had to change the translation from *dainichi* to *Deusu*. This is quite ironic since even the word Deus is borrowed from outside the Judeo-Christian tradition. Yet, missionaries accepted this as a valid way of addressing God, while the word *dainichi* was considered paganistic and even demonic. Some traditions such as the Western Christmas are not traceable back to the original Judeo–Christian traditions per se, yet they are assumed to be universally Christian. People have forgotten that they have been borrowed from other cultures, absolutized and universalized within Western Christianity, then imposed on other peoples as absolute Christian traditions. This fact alone is an indication that Western Christianity has, throughout ages, been grafted onto Western cultures. But when non-Western cultures attempt to do the same thing, they are criticized and even accused of syncretism. In fact, some aspects of Western Christianity are the product of a long-standing process of syncretism. There is actually no concept of Christianity that is totally free from this. In all of the forms in which we know it today, Christianity is the result of some sort of syncretism.

125

In short, the Christian mission in the Tokugawa Period was initially connected with colonialism and Christianity (i.e., Western religious instruction, rules, and prayers) was viewed as a substitute for local religion. Local beliefs were suppressed by missionaries and labeled as pagan. From the Japanese point of view, Christianity itself was pagan because it destroyed people's way of life and their peaceful state of mind.[50] Mase-Hasegawa believes that a dichotomy developed between European and Japanese cultures. As he writes:

> The two world-views of monotheism and poly/pantheism came into sharp contrast. The Church, as well as the missionaries, however, emphasized adoption of Western theology, the worship of 'their' God. Moreover, the West advocated the adoption of their "rites and customs". The missionary attitude thus remained the attitude of a 'giver', assuming the superiority of Western culture and Christian absoluteness. On the other hand, Japan is a metaphor for the passive reception of foreign teaching and its people recipients of Western initiatives. Thus, the image of the Church, tainted with Western conquest and theological arrogance, served to make people fear a loss of national identity.[51]

During the Meiji Period, while the official policy was tolerance, Christians experienced local opposition to evangelistic activities and pressure to renounce their faith, particularly in rural areas and in regions where Pure Land Buddhism was strong.[52] According to Ballhatchet, such opposition is not surprising, for converts were taught to reject traditional religious practices.[53]He briefly describes the effects of such refusals on both community and family levels. On the community level, there were refusals to contribute financially to local shrines or participate in religious festivals; on a family level, missionaries required that converts get rid of household shrines and Buddhist ancestral tablets as a condition of their baptism, and avoid participation in Buddhist ceremonies, including the funerals of non-Christian relatives.[54]

During the Meiji Period and beyond, Japanese theologians and thinkers such as Kanzo Uchimura, Toraji Tsukamoto, Yoshinobu Kumazawa, Kokichi Kurosaki, Seiichi Yagi, Shusaku Endo, Yoji Inoue, Mitsuo Fukuda, Yasuo Furuya, Noriyuki Miyake, Arimasa Kubo and many others attempted to contextualize the Christian message. Some of them have published books and articles for the specifically for the purpose of dialogue with Western Christians because missionaries were insensitive to Japanese culture and to religious belief.

Yoshinobu Kumazawa suggests that in the past, the Western styles of missionary work caused the non-Western world to believe that God's action toward the world is always mediated by the Western church, that God's work in non-Christian countries is mediated only by so-called Christian countries, and that Christianity is to be exported from Christian countries and implanted in non-Christian ones.[55] Kumazawa observes that this has created many problems in the history of missions, because it has led to the mistaken thought

127

that the so-called Christian countries are superior to non-Christian ones. The fatal flaw here is the presumption that God could not work directly in non-Christian countries without the mediation of Christian societies,[56] Japan being no exception. From the sixteenth century onward, missionaries from various Western church traditions and denominations were active in Japan. Their approach to the culture was blatantly ethnocentric and systematically destructive.

As John Parratt states, "if economic and political disruption resulted from Western imperialism, the demonization of indigenous cultures was more likely to be the result of European Christian missions. This happened most dramatically with traditional or folk cultures, from which the majority of Christian converts were drawn. Popular Hindu 'idolatry' or African 'fetishism' became frequent themes, especially for Christian missionaries who were eager to gain support from their Western churches. These forms of religiosity were demonized by the use of emotive and pejorative terminology. Little attempt was made to understand the kind of spirituality, which had given rise to these forms of religion.[57]

Generally speaking, the Western church has not succeeded in transmitting the gospel within the cultural context of Japan. Dean Flemming is correct when he suggests that the church must be shaped not only by what the New Testament says, but by what it does, namely by the process of contextualizing its theology.[58]

According to Sherrill, Western missionaries who came to Japan after World War II had difficulty understanding the group-orientation of Japanese society. Sherrill argues that nurturing group solidarity in the process of their evangelistic work was not something they gave serious attention. Churches, whether Roman Catholic or Protestant, often sought to convert the intellectual elite, who seemed the least bound by the constraints of Japanese society and tradition. The social and political consequence of this was, however, that churches often became gathering places for somewhat isolated—albeit highly educated—individuals.[59]

In some cases, missionaries use strategies that are more directly offensive than defensive, especially where custom and tradition are concerned, as Peter Clift observes. He calls them "rejectionists," especially when it comes to customs and traditions. Rejectionists feel that the whole set of Japanese customs are inevitably idolatrous, and ought to be rejected wholesale. Clift believes that they reject many things in Japanese culture that are, in fact, morally neutral.[60] The zeal of such missionaries in Japan as well as their heartfelt concerns for the Japanese people are commendable, yet when it comes to cultural sensitivity, they might be better advised to find ways to avoid confrontational discussions concerning customs and traditions.

A second group missionaries is described by Clift as "conformists." They opt for total conformity to the surrounding society. They want to be tolerant, and to give no offense whatever, so they simply perform many of the practices that the society as a whole does—they just give these practices a Christian name. A third group of missionaries are said to practice creative adaption.[61]

Kenny Joseph challenges missionaries regarding why they do not offer funeral services for those who are even not Christians and who have no concept of life after death. He takes it to be a

129

troublesome fact that many missionaries say they cannot do these things for a Buddhist who has not been saved. Concerning the Christian wedding ceremony, Joseph argues that the Christian church in Japan blundered when, at the end of the 1970s, the Christian wedding boom started. In his view, instead of opening the churches to non-Christians and offering them counseling and weddings, they shut them out. The pastors locked the doors, and said that only our Christian members (bokyokaiin) can be married in a church.[62] Joseph argues that the missionaries sent them away to hotels and to thousands of newly built, million dollar-wedding chapels since these had been built by non-Christians. Not a dime was spent from any missionary's budget.[63]

In the view of Emi Mase-Hasegawa, another crucial factor in all of this is "the lack of contacts or understanding between lay Japanese Christians and doctrinal Western theology. The popular religious sensitivity or social structure of Japan was hardly thematized by the missionary. After the defeat in the war, many Japanese suffered a crisis of belief but Christian doctrines did not meet their spiritual need because the Japanese public regarded Christianity as a religion of the conquerors. Thus, the post-war Christian generation demanded the liberation of Japanese theology from Western captivity."[64] For instance, Yoji Inoue criticized Western methods of transplanting Christianity to Japan and argued for a transformation of Christianity in social context. He claimed that the way of preaching in Japan for the hundred years after Meiji Period tended to create a European cultural region within Japan — and this to too great a degree. It cut the Japanese off from their Japanese culture and roots, and transformed them into Europeans. Father Inoue challenges Western missionaries by suggesting that, despite all of their efforts, Japanese have never become Europeans, and they have never wanted to. He argues that they seemed to have accepted many things from the European except Christianity.[65] As he states,

> Christianity in Japan after the Meiji period, both Catholic and Protestant, has been trying to transplant a large tree, European Christianity, which grew up on European soil, directly on the Japanese soil, instead of planting a seedling. Therefore Christianity, in general, has been far from keeping in touch with connecting with the Japanese mental climate and soil, admitting the exception of Uchimura Kanzo by whom Christianity connected to Bushido, the Japanese chivalry. And now Shusaku Endo's recent work, "On the Coast of the Dead Sea" and "A Life of Jesus" are epoch making novels in which Christianity and Japanese mental climate and soil are definitely connected with each other for the first time, though you may approve of disapprove of the image of Jesus in them.[66]

Inoue notes that Christianity came to Japan through missionaries, who carried in their blood the history of Western culture. Accordingly, Christianity was not accepted in the way something is

131

generally accepted in Japan—it was rather forced upon the people. They were made to accept it in the same way that European people had. He, too, believes this is why the Japanese did not accept the Christianity that was offered to them by the Europeans (i.e., the West).[67]

5.5 Denominational Competition

According to Kitagawa, "the task of evangelism is interpreted by most missionaries as transplanting the Western church onto Japanese soil, including the ugly features of denominationalism—an unhappy assumption, indeed."[68] It is a fact that, during the Tokugawa Period, the Jesuits and Franciscans constantly betrayed each other. The Jesuits intrigued to have the Spaniards expelled, the Spaniards pressed for the exclusion of the Dutch. There was an ongoing rivalry between them.[69]

Even after the Tokugawa Period, competition between missionaries continued. As Kanzo Uchimura once said, "To us it makes no difference whether that man becomes a Roman Catholic, or a Greek Catholic, or a Baptist, or a Presbyterian, or a member of any one of the six hundred and more of the Christian sects and churches, which, we hear, exist in Christendom. We are thankful, yea, we rejoice, when a man is saved from his sins to a pure, humble life in Jesus Christ. But missionaries seem not to rejoice and be thankful unless a heathen is converted and he joins their own respective churches."[70] And, in 1983, Endo stated:

I am not interested in the system or hierarchy of the
church in Japan . . . As for Japan and the Japanese,
the hierarchy of the Church (a bishop or archbishop)
is really none of my concern. As long as the Church
or officials avoid confronting the issues and problems
of Japanese, they are useless... There are many
ordained Japanese, but I have little interest in those
who profess the Christian theology they learned in
the West.[71]

After World War II, the missionaries, mission organizations and
churches worked relatively closely together to break down the walls
of denominationalism. Japan Evangelical Missionary Association
(JEMA), which consists of about 2,000 missionaries who are active
in Japan, has been able to facilitate inter-denominational fellowship
in this way, to get beyond the previously existing barrier between the
evangelical and charismatic communities.[72]

What lessons are to be learned from all of this? Missionaries
have to constantly remind themselves that, in order to reach
others, they must first learn to be proper guests. We cannot come
to foreign nations with the assumption that we have everything to
teach them and they have everything to learn from us. As Father
Louis Massignon, the late French Christian priest and renowned
Islamic scholar said, "to understand the other, one does not need
to annex him but to become his guest."[73] As for the manner and
spirit of the presentation of our faith, what is of highest importance
is captured in a deeply penetrating statement made by the Bengali

poet, Rabindranath Tagore, winner of the Nobel Prize for literature in 1913: "When Christians bring their truth to a strange land, unless they bring it in the form of homage, it is not accepted and should not be.[74]"

Still, it continues to be the case that, when people become followers of Christ as a result of having been proselytized by Western missionaries, they are often told that they need to leave their cultural past behind, to disassociate themselves from their community and family, and attempt to adopt a "Christian" identity. They still are encouraged to take new Western Christian names such as John, Peter, David, Mary, and Susanna and to stop attending cultural ceremonies or participating in family religious ceremonies; instead, they celebrate Christmas by placing Christmas trees in their houses and participating in the story of Santa Claus, and celebrate Easter by painting eggs.

Lastly, it is crucial to mention that, despite some shortcomings on the part of missionaries throughout history, and despite their unfortunate connection to colonialism or their unquestioned commitment to the Western worldview, it cannot be denied that all missionaries from different traditions and denominations have played an significant role in shaping Japanese society and culture, both in the past and today. Evidence of this can still to be found today. For example, missionaries have established seminaries and trained clergy, established churches and educated local Christians, challenged some aspect of Japanese society about how to treat the poor and the untouchables (i.e., the *burakumin*), established hospitals and charitable organizations and, of course, most recently, have been intensely involved in relief work for the victims of the tsunami and earthquake of March 11, 2010. All of these are, and have been, significant contributions to life in Japan.

Notes

1   Ikuo Higashibaba, *Christianity in early modern Japan: Kirishitans belief and practice* (Leiden: Brill, 2001), xvii.

2   When he was 36 years old, Anjiro fled Japan after committing murder. He boarded a Portuguese ship heading for India. There he met Francis Xavier. Anjiro is the first-recorded Japanese convert to Christianity. During this period he learned to speak Portuguese. When the Portuguese missionaries arrived in Japan, they needed an interpreter. Even though Anjiro had intuitive intelligence, he had no educational background whatsoever. This certainly had huge implications for the introduction of Christianity into Japan. However, the missionaries' lack of knowledge of the Japanese language forced them to rely, at least initially, on Anjiro.

3   Ebisawa Arimichi, *Nihon Kirishitan Shi* (Tokyo: Hanaba Shobo, 1966), 179.

4   Urs App, "Francis Xavier's Discovery of Japanese Buddhism: A Chapter in the European Discovery of Buddhism (part 1: Before the Arrival in Japan, 1547-1549). *The Eastern Buddhist* Vol. xxx No.1 (1997), 241.

5   Olof G. Lidin, *Tanegashima: The Arrival of European in Japan* (Taylor & Francis e-Library, 2005), 119.

6   Toshifumi Uemura, "The Way to State Shinto In Comparison with Shrine Shinto", in *The Unseen Face of Japan: Culturally Appropriate Communication of the Gospel*, ed. Cynthia Dufty. PDF Version 1.1. (Tokyo: Hayama Missionary Seminar Report 1988), 8.

7   Higashibaba, 35–36.

8   Atsuyoshi Fujiwara, "Theology of culture in a Japanese context:
a believers' church perspective"(PhD diss., Durham University,
1999), 209.

9   Ibid.

10   Ibid.

11   Ernest W. Clement, *Christianity in Modern Japan* (Philadelphia:
American Baptist Publication Society, 1905), 28.

12   Furuya, 142.

13   Fujiwara, 212.

14   Ibid.

15   Fujiwara, 222.

16   Ibid.

17   Sherrill, 164.

18   Ibid.

19   Joseph M. Kitagawa, "The Contemporary Religious Situation
in Japan," *Japanese Religions* II 2–3 (1961), 40–41.

20   Lee, 102.

21   Shu Kishida, *A Place for Apology: War, Guilt and US-Japan Relations*
      (Lanham: Hamilton Books, 2004), 65,

22   Boxer, 146.

23   Ibid.

24   Boxer, 148.

25   Boxer, 138.

26   Mary Bernard, *Japan's Martyr Church* (Exeter: Catholic
      Records Press, 1926), 20.

27   Kiri Paramore, *Ideology and Christianity in Japan.*
      (Oxon: Routledge, 2009),10.

28   Ibid.

29   Paramore, 11.

30   Monika Schrimpf, "The Pro-and Anti-Christian Writings of Fukan
      Fabian (1565-1621)" In *Japanese Religions* Vol. 33, No.1 & 2
      (Kyoto: Center for the Study of Japanese Religions, July 2008), 39.

31   George Elison, *Deus Destroyed: The Image of Christianity in
      Early Modern Japan.* (Massachusetts: Harvard University Asia
      Center, 1988), 289.

32   Elison, 51.

33   Ballhatchet, 36.

34 Ballhatchet, 37.

35 Ballhatchet, 42.

36 Hiroshi Miura, *The Life and Thought of Kanzo Uchimura 1861–1930* (Cambridge: Wm B. Eerdmans, 1996), 73.

37 Miura, 74.

38 Miura, 75.

39 Miura, 76.

40 Kishida, 36

41 Ibid.

42 Mullins 1998, 38.

43 Robert Kerby, "Is it a scandal that Gen. MacArthur thought Christianity would help Japan?" http://blog.beliefnet.com/on_ the_front_lines_of_the_culture_wars/2011/06/scandal- general-douglas-macarthur-thought-christianity-would-help-japan. html#ixzz24JbubTHy.

44 Jun Eto, "The censorship operation in occupied Japan," in *Press Control Around the World*, ed. Jane Curry and Joan Dassin, (New York, N.Y.: Praeger Publishers, 1982). 235-53.

45 Naoko Kato, *War Guilt and Postwar Japan* Donald Thurston, (M.A. Thesis, The University of British Colombia, 2002),9. Kato refers to Jun Eto, *Tozasareta Gengo Kukan (Contained Realm of Discourse: Censorship Operation by the Occupational Forces and Postwar*

Japan). 2d ed., (Tokyo: Bungeishunj, 1998).

46   Ibid.

47   Miyake, 40.

48   P. G. Hiebert, "Critical Contextualization" in *Missiology: An International Review* 1984,12(3): 288.

49   Toshifumi Uemura, "The Way to State Shinto In Comparison with Shrine Shinto" in *Hayama Missionary Seminar Report* 1988, PDF Version 1.1, November 2008, 8.

50   Hasegawa, 166-67.

51   Hasegawa, 167.

52   Ballhatchet, 37.

53   Ibid.

54   Ibid.

55   Gerald H. Anderson (ed.) *Asian Voices in Christian Theology,* (New York: Orbis Books, 1976), 204.

56   Ibid.

57   John Parratt (ed), *An Introduction To Third World Theologies,* (Cambridge: Cambridge University Press, 2004), 5.

58   Dean Flemming, *Contextualization in the New Testament: Patterns for Theology and Mission*, (Downers Grove: Intervarsity Press, 2005), 296.

59   Sherrill, 167.

60   Peter Clift, "Uh Oh, What Now? I have to Conduct a Funeral!"
Funerals as Wonderful Opportunities to Proclaim the Gospel of
Hope in *The Unseen Face of Japan: Culturally Appropriate
Communication of the Gospel.* Hayama Seminary Annual Report,
Tokyo (2001), 99.

61   Clift, 100.

62   Kenny Joseph, "Response to Peter Clift's presentation, Funerals
as Wonderful Opportunities" in *The Unseen Face of Japan: Culturally
Appropriate Communication of the Gospel.* Hayama Seminary
Annual Report, Tokyo (2001), 118

63   Ibid.

64   Hasegawa, 121.

65   Yoji Inoue, *The Faces of Jesus in Japan* translated by Hisako
Akamatsu (Tokyo: Kindai-Bungeisha, 1994), 65.

66   Ibid.

67   Ibid.

68   Mullins, 1998, 35.

69   Sansom, 426.

70   Mullins, 1998, 29.

71   Hasegawa, 126. Hasegawa refers to Endo's *Watashi ni totte
Kami towa* (God for Me) Tokyo: Koubundo 1983/1988.

72   Minoru Okuyama, "Japanese Challenges: Buddhism, Shintoism
and Others" paper presented at *TOKYO 2010 Global Mission
Consultation: From Edinburgh 1910 to Tokyo 2010*
(May 13, 2010), 62.

73   Paul Gordon Chandler, *Pilgrims of Christ on the Muslim Road:
Exploring a New Path Between Two Faiths* (Lanham: Rowman &
Littlefield Publishing Group, 2007), 93.

74   Ibid.

Why is **Christianity** Not Widely
Believed in Japan?

Chapter 6

SOCIETAL FACTORS

The way Japanese society is structured is one of the factors why Christianity has not yet taken root in Japan. In the following paragraphs, I therefore discuss some aspects of Japanese society that are significant for this issue. According to the 2010 edition of *Operation World*, its annual growth rate is –0.2 percent, which is lower than the 0.1 percent reported in the 2001 edition of this same publication.[1]

Like any post-modern nation, Japan is a very dynamic and vibrant society. To the eyes of an outsider, Japanese society may appear like any Western society with a high level of technological achievement. However, the Japanese have somewhat different ways of organizing their life than the Western societies do.

6.1 Social Status

If one visits Japan for business, one may notice that when two people meet for the first time they immediately exchange business cards. This is an important custom in Japan because it informs the other person of your status. Generally, it allows them to know where they stand relative to others. The information on the business card will determine which mannerisms and forms of social treatment are appropriate. Even the language used during the conversation will be based on the relative positions of the two people. The person of lower rank will, for example, bow more deeply than the other. How do the Japanese conceive of social stratification? The Japanese equivalents of the words "class" and "stratum" (*kaikyu* and *kaiso*, respectively) are both translations based on their English equivalents. Still, the Japanese have a clear conception of social stratification, even if their notion of it may seem to be borrowed from Western culture.[2]

There are several Japanese terms for social stratification. *Kaku* denotes a finite series of ranks. It is a generic term that can be applied to a wide range of ranking systems.[3] *Mibun* implies the status into which a person is born. The term *kakei* (family line) has a similar connotation, but it emphasizes lineage and pedigree to a greater degree. In contrast, *chii* refers to the status a person achieves over time.[4] In her book, *Japanese Society*, Nakane Chie explains that groups in Japan may be identified by applying two criteria: one is based on the individual's common attributes and the other on position within a given social framework.[5] A framework may be a locality, an institution, or a particular relationship that unites a set of individuals within a group. In all cases, it provides a criterion for defining a boundary and so establishes a common basis for a set of individuals who are located within, or involved in, a class.[6] In contrast to this, the term "attribute" refers to one's being a member of a definite group or caste. Attribute may be acquired not only by birth, but also by achievement.[7] These criteria serve to identify individuals in a certain group. That group can then be classified within the whole of society even though it may or may not have a particular function of its own.[8] Generally, throughout his or her lifetime, a person is placed within various social frameworks

144

and defined by certain attributes. The most important of these are
family, neighborhood, and educational and occupational affiliations.

6.2 The Japanese Family

I commence my analysis of Japanese family by considering children.
From an early age, they are trained to be aware of hierarchy and
to find their place both in the home and outside of it. Children are
trained first to think and act within the group to which they belong,
and then to act individually. That is they are raised to be group-
oriented rather than self-oriented. Consequently, they may belong to
different groups with different contexts. They have to act for the sake
of harmony of the *uchi* to which they belong. This may consist of their
siblings at home, their friends at kindergarten, or their classmates
at school. The importance of group harmony was emphasized in
chapter three. Group harmony forms the basic worldview from which
a person operates throughout his or her life, and, as discussed in
chapter three, this can constitute an obstacle to the acceptance and
practice of Christianity.

In nuclear families, especially those in which the husband
works for a major corporation, the wife commonly stays at home
and looks after the home and the small children. She is usually
entrusted with the family finances as well. Some women take this
role so seriously that they are called 'professional housewives'. [9]
They have considerable input into their children's education, diet,
and general well-being. However, the duties of the wife do not just
consist of caring for her household, husband, and children. The fact
that Japanese people (especially women) have high life expectancy

actually makes life harder for wives than for husbands because they are expected to care for elderly family members who live longer and require special care and attention. These responsibilities make it difficult for them to hold full-time jobs. Because there is insufficient aid available for working parents and also not enough daycare centers and pre-schools in Japan, and since it is expected that family life will interfere with the husband's work, mothers frequently choose to quit their jobs for the sake of educating and raising their children.

Japanese families are often referred to as "fatherless," a term that describes two common situations: families in which the father has little time to be with his family because he is obligated to long work days, and families in which he is absent due to divorce or separation. Both situations are alarmingly common in Japan. Long working hours and after-work drinks with colleagues mean that fathers are away from home most of the day. On average, they spend 17 minutes a day with their children and no additional time helping to looking after them.[10]

Generally speaking, mothers are often occupied with various activities associated with the education of their children and also with neighborhood activities; fathers are busy working and participating in the workplace community. Having so little time to spend with family is not a uniquely Japanese problem—indeed it is one that has developed in many (post) modern societies. but it is nevertheless, the families in Japan may not actually have the freedom to choose an organized religion such as Christianity given the demands it places on them socially (e.g., social activities and

146

church services).

6.3 Neighborhood Communities

According to Joy Hendry, after the family, the next important social unit in Japanese society is the neighborhood.[11] Even though every neighborhood is different, there are certain expectations among neighbors, and they seem to be characteristically Japanese. They can be used as a yardstick for analysis even when the expectations conform little with actual behavior.[12] Hendry describes various forms of neighborly cooperation and joint activities involving children and adults. These are all part of the neighborhood experience, and people are expected to participate in different activities.

In both rural and urban Japan, neighborhoods play a very important role when it comes to social control, social reciprocity, and neighborhood moral, spiritual, and practical duties carried out by members of the neighborhood community (i.e., households). This can vary from taking care of the children, participating in activities for children and the elderly, to those relating to shrines or temples and religious or folkloric festivals.

In rural Japan, a further task to which the entire community is expected to contribute is the care of the places of worship such as shrines situated within village boundaries. Groups of houses are assigned responsibilities for this on a rotating schedule. Responsibilities vary from cleaning the buildings and maintaining the grounds to celebrating the seasonal festivals associated with the sacred places. All such activities are taken to be simultaneously neighborly duties and religious ones.[13] They are so important that

147

even houses that have converted to a new religion (e.g., Christianity) are expected to take part in them. If people refuse, they are ostracized for their failure to co-operate. Formal ostracism is used occasionally in Japanese communities to express disapproval of some action as antisocial.[14]

Whether the community is urban or rural, Japan has a rich array of models for neighborly interaction. It is not difficult to handle local demands based on these models, be they ideological or practical. The principles of knowing and caring about one's neighbors have long been strongly upheld in Japanese community life, and evidence seems to suggest that these are still viewed as important.[15] In newer neighborhoods and in apartment complexes, women in particular complain of loneliness and lack of interaction with neighbors. Elsewhere, there is no doubt that such women draw on the traditions of neighborly interaction to overcome isolation.[16]

6.4 Japanese Working Life

The Japanese are known to be an industrious people. They work long hours and are almost never absent from their jobs. This is the image many have of the Japanese labor force. A Japanese employee is generally referred to as *salaryman*, an English loan word that has entered their language.[17]

Japanese companies function quite differently from their European and American counterparts, although this has changed in recent years. Japan basically has a lifetime employment system: workers are generally employed by the same company for their entire professional lives. A unique Japanese company culture has been developed based on this principle. Schools and universities often have contracts with companies that ensure that, immediately after graduating, some of their students will enter these companies. For decades, this was how employees were recruited. It was one of the reasons why Japan had a low unemployment rate in the past.[18]

Working in Japan not only requires doing your job skillfully, it also requires fitting in with the company culture. The Japanese feel it is important to love their company. In Japan, it has been believed that the morals and mental attitudes of the individual have an important bearing on productivity. Company loyalty has long been highly valued.[19] A man may be an excellent technician, but if his way of thinking and morals differ from those of the company, the company will not hesitate to dismiss him. Men who enter a company after working for another one at a comparatively advanced stage in their working lives tend to be difficult to mold and their loyalties are therefore suspect.[20] Since this lifetime employment system is a family-like group, it affects the private lives of the employees. This is crucial for group unity because the individual's total emotional participation in a group helps form a close-knit group.[21]

Companies provide various services and benefits for their employees, such as pensions, health care, and often accommodation (e.g., dormitories for unmarried workers, apartments for families, and even large houses for senior employees).[22] In return, employees are expected to perform to the very best of their ability. They are also expected to take few holidays and spend their leisure time with their colleagues drinking in local bars, playing sport together, or going on office trips. Within this group-oriented system, there are peer

149

level and junior/senior interactions on the individual level. In most companies, the president is considered the father of the house. As such, he has the right to intervene in the private lives of his employees by doing things such as finding a spouse for someone.

Another aspect of Japanese working life concerns the company one belongs to. Japanese people do not ask what you do for a living; rather, they want to know which company you work for. Working in Japan means belonging to a group that is your working family, especially for the major corporations or institutions. Each institution may also have its own song or anthem, so singing it promotes a sense of unity among employees and employers.

Most Japanese companies have created their own sort of company religion with rites and ceremonies designed to strengthen the work atmosphere and reinforce a sense of social unity. Most Japanese companies do not want to employ people who are members of religious organizations because they feel that their loyalties will be divided. Thomas P. Rohlen conducted a case study of a Japanese bank and its management and working culture. In his book, *For Harmony and Strength*, he describes the ceremonies that were conducted there. He discusses, for example, the various catechisms that are recited during the entrance ceremony for new employees. Employees sing the company anthem together. [23]

Rohlen also found out that the bank did not want to employ members of 'new religions', because these demand considerable time and effort from their members.[24] This is not because the bank considers these religions inherently bad; on the contrary, it views many of them as being positive moral forces. But it does not want its employees to have divided loyalties. Furthermore, the religious behavior of the parents of a potential employee is considered important: the bank is not interested in employing the children of religious zealots.[25] Japanese companies have created their own religion and what they practice is no less a religion than that practiced by religious organizations. The habit of not employing people who are members of a religious organization indicates that some degree of competition exists between the 'company religion' and conventional religions.

On the other hand, it is important to note that Japanese business does not consist solely of major enterprises and institutions. Most companies are medium or small enterprises such as family businesses. These differ from the large ones in several ways. Loyalty to the company and the group is still important for medium and small companies; however, they are unable to provide the same benefits as large companies. This does not mean that loyalty is not strong within them. On the contrary, because of their smaller size, group unity is actually more important than it is for larger companies.

Japanese society is changing rapidly and this is affecting working life in the country. There is now a growing shift away from a lifetime employment system to a performance-based one. A survey by the Ministry of Labor revealed that the incomes of college graduates aged 40–45 varied more widely in 1998 than in 1993. Many claim that this growing income range reflects the new preference for performance-based remuneration.[26] Performance-based systems no longer pay employees on the basis of seniority and length of time at

151

a company, but rather on performance and achievement.

Another tendency in Japanese working culture is for young people to work part-time and have more than one job. Such people are called *furiitaa*, which means 'free person' since they are free from the constraints imposed by the lifestyle of a typical salaryman. According to Matsumoto, "the stereotype of the Japanese salaryman who is willing to sacrifice himself and his family, who is happy to be a worker bee for the sake of company and country, and who does not relish rewards based on individual achievements is more myth than reality, especially among younger workers."[27]

6.5 Education in Japan

It is widely believed that the Japanese educational structure is of a 'tournament' type in which losers who have failed in their teens are virtually unable to take up the same challenge in life.[28] One of the biggest concerns for Japanese adolescents is their performance in the educational system, where they often experience significant pressure from parents and society in general. In extreme cases, this pressure starts even before they enter preschool—they sometimes have to pass an entrance exam even to get into the best preschool. Preschool prepares children for the entrance exam for the best kindergarten, which, in turn, prepares them for the entrance exam to the best primary school, junior high school, high school, and eventually the best university.

Another source of pressure comes from peers. They can harass or bully some students for various reasons, including obesity, ethnicity, or a perceived lack of intelligence, sports ability,

152

or money. Bullying seems to have replaced examination pressure as a major cause of child suicide and school refusal in recent reports, and special centers have been set up to provide phone-in help for victims.[29]

The Japanese educational system has generated a great deal of debate among scholars and educators. Some praise it while others criticize it. Some believe that the strong emphasis placed on the group loyalty and unity causes the individual aspects of a child's development to be ignored. Others suggest that such a highly authoritarian educational system can frustrate children and can even lead some to commit suicide.[30]

Once students have been accepted into a school, the Japanese very skillfully avoid overt competition in order to maintain harmony among them and downplay differences in ability. In fact, almost no one fails. However, the ruthless entrance examinations represent competition at its worst, and they cast a shadow on a young person's life long in advance of adulthood. Indeed, they subject students to severe pressure throughout most of their schooling and distort the content of their education. Much of the training in senior high schools is devoted not to learning as such, but to preparing students to pass university entrance examinations.[31] On the other hand, some believe that the Japanese education system is unique and teaches children about the importance of unity, harmony, and discipline. In the West, this would be termed moral education.

Further, going to school in Japan is not just about acquiring knowledge. Japanese education emphasizes moral training—such character traits as diligence, endurance, deciding to do hard things,

153

wholehearted dedication to a cause, and social co-operation. For example, children are organized into cleaning groups that have to work together to keep their school clean. Physical education is also very important. School children have to exercise every morning.[32]

The Japanese educational system is, as noted above, group oriented, and the cohesion of the group is more important than individual competition in classes. Students are discouraged from asking their teachers many questions because they may be perceived as disrupting the group for their own personal interests. The group is also emphasized over the individual in sports. Once again, it is noticeable that harmony and group play an important role in the education system of the Japanese, and choosing to be active in a religious group (e.g., Christianity) can disturb the group harmony and possibly adversely influence the personal educational endeavors of the students.

6.6 Demographic Shifts

In 2009, only 13 percent of Japan's population was under 15 years old. According to Jeff Kingston, the nation's low fertility rate is due to the fact that women find it difficult to juggle work and family responsibilities. Kingston writes:

> As a result, many working women are delaying or forgoing marriage altogether, while a growing number of those who marry choose not to have children. As attitudes and social norms have changed, and lifestyles diversify, getting married and having children

is no longer the default option it once was. Women who are now enjoying greater social and economic freedom wonder if having kids is really what they want, and consider carefully what they stand to lose by raising a family, especially given that their husbands (and their employers) continue to shift most of the child-rearing burden on them.[33]

The combination of the low fertility rate and long life expectancy (86.05 years for women and 79.29 years for men in 2009) means that Japan is becoming a geriatric society. Such longevity is a consequence of healthy eating habits among the middle aged and elderly.[34]

Currently, a mere 0.22 percent of Japan's population attends Christian services. Such figures raise serious concerns about the future of the Christian church in Japan. Some predict that, in 20 years' time, nearly 50 percent of the country's churches will be vacant.[35] Japan's elderly church members will have passed away and no young people will be available to replenish their congregations. Furthermore, attracting new members is like trying "to draw water with a bamboo basket" (an ancient Japanese proverb). As far as the 9,000-member Reformed Church in Japan is concerned, the future is now. If the existing denominations are to survive, the gospel must be instilled in their young members whose leadership can form the foundation of Japan's reformed faith.[36]

6.7 Materialism and Modern Society

Japan is also an entertainment and leisure-oriented society. The Japanese social life is very stressful, thus people find refuge in all types of entertainment and pleasure. This fact defines all aspects of life, such as food, shelter, clothing, and shopping, as well as new media technologies (e.g., mass journalism, radio, film, and television), new genres of expressive culture in anime, manga, and music, and expanded leisure activities, including sports, travel, hobbies, and other forms of entertainment. The sincerely hard-working Japanese are often too busy to pay attention to Christianity.[37]

The stressful social lifestyle have discouraged those who are considering to become Christians. Of those who have been baptized, half leave their churches within two or three years.[38] Materialism thus dominates the ambition of younger Japanese. Some Japanese reject Christianity because they relate being a Christian to attending church on Sundays—and most of them cannot afford to do this. According to Operation World (2010), even Christians do not regularly attend church: "Church attendance is low; less than half of church members regularly attend. Often Christians are influenced by Buddhist/Shinto religions, which have no regular attendance requirements, and they carry this thinking into Christian activities."[39]

George S. Noss, for instance, a Japan-born son of US missionaries, and himself a missionary in rural Japan for 11 years during the 1930s and teacher of Japanese at Columbia University, stated decades ago that, to the Japanese, cherry blossoms are the "symbols of the supreme beauty of sacrifice." The Japanese, he declares, never feel at home in "the ugly and incongruous Western

156

chapel," or "even in a fine Gothic church." He recommended that future Christian churches in Japan be built in "the shrine form of architecture, with its clean lines and austere beauty." He would even have them include the Buddhist torii (ceremonial gateway). Moreover, churches should be situated on streets, but be "hidden in groves of trees with torn and mossy stone steps, fountains of water, and old flowering shrubs." He also recommends drastic changes to the interiors of typical Christian buildings.[40] This could attract the busy Japanese and enable them to find rest and peace in the Christian spirit within a native Japanese setting.

Further, as I mentioned earlier, most Japanese fathers are spending increasingly less time with their family and more with their company community. They hardly have sufficient time or energy to practice Christianity, especially attend church regularly. Operation World cites the following in its report: "The drive for success and desire to satisfy the demands of employers make it hard for men to openly identify with and become active in a church. On average, women attendees outnumber men 7 to 1."[41] On the other hand, the Japanese companies cannot afford to have their employees be an active member of any religious group (e.g., Christianity).

As described above, the demographic situation of Japan is hindering the growth of Christianity in the sense that those who are already Christians are dying out and the young people are occupied with various social responsibilities from childhood, to adolescence, to parenting or providing for the needs of the family. This demographic decline is not only affecting the number of Christians in Japan, it is also having drastic consequences for the future of Christian leadership. "Seventy percent of the pastors are over 50 years old. Leadership transition can be difficult and sensitive in a society that so reveres the elderly."[42] It also means that there is a need to train new evangelists and pastors who can share the gospel with Japanese. Thus, Bible training for Christian workers is crucial.

6.8 Minority Image

In Japan, Christianity is not only associated with Western missionaries, but also with other ethnic minorities such as Koreans, and Overseas Migrant Workers from other countries such as the Philippines. Japan has five major minority groups: *burakumin* (a caste-like group), Okinawans (an indigenous race), Ainu (an indigenous race), Japanese-born Koreans, and migrant workers from other countries. The discrimination that many of these groups encounter has its origins in the imperialist and feudal periods in Japan's history. In the eighth century, the Japanese expanded their territory into the regions of the Ainu and Okinawans, two indigenous races whose lands have now been incorporated into modern Japan. The term *burakumin* ('hamlet people') refers to Japan's traditional 'unclean' caste, which is also known as *eta* ('filthy mass') and *hinin* ('non-human').

During the Tokugawa Period, "*burakumin* were associated with defiling occupations, such as burying the dead and tanning the hides of animals. The former is polluting from a Shinto viewpoint, the latter from a Buddhist perspective."[43] Still today, the *burakumin* are a separate class, whatever their occupations. 'Regular Japanese' are most careful not to marry them and 'pollute' their own bloodlines.

158

One of the factors working against integration for these people is the system of family registration, by which 'outcaste' people can often be recognized on the basis of their areas of origin.[44]

The Ainu are the aborigines of northern Japan. The Ainu may suffer a similar fate as *burakumin*, although there has recently been evidence that they are benefiting from a worldwide interest in the rights of indigenous people and re-acquiring some of their cultural heritage.[45]

There are approximately 700,000 North and South Koreans in Japan today,[46] most of whom were born and grew up in Japan. Many belong to families who have lived in Japan for three or even four generations. However, since Japanese nationality is based on lineage, these Korean descendants are not automatically awarded Japanese citizenship, something which is very hard to understand from a Western perspective. A third- or fourth-generation African in Europe or the US is automatically a citizen, but this is not the case in Japan: once a Korean, always a Korean. There are also Koreans, who have become naturalized and hold Japanese passports, but their names have been rendered Japanese and it is not easy to discover that they are Korean. Some children of Korean–Japanese marriages have become Japanese nationals as well. Many Korean pastors and missionaries serve the Christian church in Japan and many of these churches are also attended by Japanese Christians. In major cities such as Tokyo, there are many international churches where Koreans, Africans, and other ethnic groups worship alongside fellow Japanese Christians.

Japanese prejudice toward minorities is strongly rooted in

cultural beliefs. In general, prejudice is based on the claim that whatever is from the outside *(soto)* is ought not be not accepted. Minorities are not full members of the stratified, Japanese social system; yet they often fall outside the mainstream and can therefore be considered strange or weird. Therefore, foreigners who come to Japan to do low profile work, the *burakumin*, those belonging to New Religions, or to Christianity are considered outré. Protective parents often employ private detectives to check up on a child's potential spouse, to determine whether he or she has any *buraku* or Korean blood.[47] The average Japanese relates to the Christianity or even to the thought of conversion with a sense of discomfort. Family or peer pressure will certainly intervene to discourage them from converting or even from associating with Christians.

6.9 Class Dichotomies

According to Mullins, Christianity in Japan has long been considered a demanding religion, one that is largely related to intellectualism and the educated white-collar middle class. This image is related to the decision of the earliest Protestant missionaries to concentrate their efforts on Japanese from the samurai class.[48] This has, however, been changing, according to Mullins a number of other indigenous movements have made similar cultural adaptations and attracted members from among the less educated strata of society.[49]

In the Meiji Period, the samurai class, the most literate and intellectual stratum of Japanese society at the time, was overrepresented in the churches: the mere 5 percent of the total Japanese population in the 1880s and 1890s who were of samurai origin accounted for approximately 30 percent of total membership in the Protestant churches.[50] In interviews I conducted with some Japanese pastors, they confirmed this intellectual and non-intellectual dichotomy. One of my respondents made the following observation: "I think many Christians have high-social status in mainline churches, they are of the older generation. But nowadays, there are many low social status people in many churches, especially among the Pentecostal churches or new-type churches from USA. These churches are more powerful than mainline churches."

This dichotomy in social status, high versus low, may also represent a barrier to the average Japanese citizen becoming a Christian. Too much intellectualism makes it hard for Japanese to understand the Christian message and they hesitate to associate with highly educated Christians; on the other hand, some Christians relate to the less intellectual, so-called low-profile citizens who are members of minorities. This may make it difficult for the Japanese people to accept and practice Christianity, for they may not like to be associated with either social group. Further, as mentioned earlier, women outnumber men in the churches—and this to such a degree that Christianity could be considered the religion of women. For this reason as well, the average Japanese may not like to associate with it.

Some aspects of Japanese society have been described above; hence I may now draw some conclusions as to why there are so few who convert to Christianity. First, the average Japanese is already fully occupied with a plethora of activities, and these may hinder him or her from even considering becoming a Christian.

The majority of the people of Japan are very busy living their lives, maintaining social harmony, and fulfilling their duties to society. Further, the Japanese are wary of Christianity with minorities and of certain social classes, so demographic factors play an important role in explaining why Christianity is not advancing in Japan.

Lastly, as Sherrill rightfully indicates, that Christianity in post World War II also had to confront the phenomenon of rapid secularization in Japan. People had been bound to religious traditions and observances that cast a veil of holiness over natural objects, persons, social structures, and other phenomena. The processes of secularization stripped this away and set people free from the bondage to traditional religion.[51] The Japanese were therefore free to pursue economic development through capitalism and they relegated religion to the rather limited activity of maintaining various rituals and customs. The pursuit of material goods captured the interest of society, and the church and its evangelistic campaigns lost their appeal.[52]

It is important to mention here that, even though secularization did influence change in traditional religious views and practices of Japanese people, it did not succeed in fully changing the Japanese worldviews as it is described in chapter three. The concepts such as the group wa, uchi-soto, giri, honne-tatemae and amae are still visible and vibrant in the secularized Japanese society.

The next chapter will discuss political factors related to the central question of my research. It will seek to determine whether or not politics has played (or still plays) a role in the way Japanese view Christianity.

Notes

1   Mandryk, 489.

2   Yoshio Sugimoto, *An Introduction to Japanese Society*
(Cambridge: Cambridge University Press, 2003), 56.

3   Ibid.

4   Ibid.

5   Nakane, 1.

6   Ibid.

7   Nakane, 2.

8   Ibid.

9   Hendry, 37.

10   Masako Ishii-Kuntz, "Japanese fathers' involvement in childcare",
a power point presentation". Power point Presentation at University
of California, Riverside: department of sociology, 2004).

11   Hendry, 57.

12   Ibid.

13   Hendry, 62.

14   Hendry, 62-3.

15   Hendry, 77.

16   Hendry, 77-8.

17   Sugimoto,40.

18   Hendry, 156.

19   Nakane,16.

20   Ibid.

21   Nakane,19.

22   Hendry,160.

23   Thomas P. Rohlen, *For Harmony and Strength: Japanese White-collar Organization in Anthropological Perspective* (Berkley: University of California Press, 1974), 35.

24   Rohlen,72.

25   Ibid.

26   Linda S. Wojtan "Exploring contemporary Japanese society" in Japan Digest www.japandigest.com

27   David Matsumoto, *The New Japan: Debunking Seven Cultural Stereotypes* (Yarmouth: Intercultural Press, Inc., 2002), 74.

28   Sugimoto, 116.

29   Hendry, 91.

30   Hendry, 106.

31   Reischauer and Craig, 166.

32   Kaori H. Okano, "School Culture" in *The Cambridge Companion to Modern Japanese Culture*, ed. Yoshio Sugimoto (Port Melbourne: Cambridge University Press: 2009),79.

33   Jeff Kingston, *Contemporary Japan: History, Politics, and Social Change since 1980s* (West Sussex: Wiley-Blackwell, 2010), 44.

34   Kingston, 48.

35   Monir Hossain Moni, "Christianity's Failure to Thrive in Today's Japan" (Paper, Tokyo: Hitotsubashi University, Dept. of International and Asia-Pacific Studies, 2004).

36   Ibid.

37   Mandryk, 491.

38   Ibid.

39   Mandryk, 492.

40   "Christ in Japan" Times Magazine (July 31, 1944), http://www.time.com/time/magazine/article/0,9171,775098,00.html.

41   Mandryk, 492.

42   Ibid.

43   Hendry, 82.

44   Ibid.

45   Ibid.

46   Jeffrey Hays, "Koreans in Japan: Discrimination, Citizenship, North Korean Schools and Japanese Wives in North Korea" in Facts & Details: http://factsanddetails.com/japan php?itemid=635&catid=18 last modified in January 2013.

47   Nobutaka Oba, "I have no intention of discrimination, but . . . " –Toward a Sociology of Knowledge about Discrimination" (Article, Monash University, 2013), 10.

48   Mullins 1998, 95.

49   Mullins 1998, 97.

50   Mullins 1998, 95.

51   Sherrill, 167.

52   Ibid.

Chapter 7

POLITICAL FACTORS

Since the arrival of Roman Catholicism in Japan in the sixteenth century, Christianity has generally been regarded as an intrusive force, indeed it has often been referred to as evil religion.[1] Mullins suggests that the macro-political relations that defined various stages of the transplantation process have undoubtedly shaped the perception of Christianity as a deviant religion, one connected to aggressive foreign powers who have designs upon Japan.[2] According to Mullins "this is how Protestant Christianity was largely perceived when missionaries arrived from North America and Europe at the end of the Tokugawa Period. As latecomers to Japan's religious scene, both Catholic and Protestant churches have experienced considerable difficulty in ridding themselves of their reputation as foreign religions."[3]

7.1 Historical Context

As I indicated in chapter two, by the end of the sixteenth century, Japan was undergoing a process of social and political unification; a national state was being formed. During the Tokugawa regime when Japan had been more thoroughly unified, the warlords who were anti-European would come to support the Shogun in an effort to ban the Europeans and their religion. They were not comfortable with Christians who would likely remain loyal to an external religious and political figures such as the Pope and the Spanish king.[4]

Christianity that was initially brought to Japan by late sixteenth century—Catholic missionaries was theoretically "politics-free." In reality, however, as elsewhere during that period, the missionary endeavors of Western Christianity ran in parallel with the political ambitions of Western nations in colonizing the world, and they showed less respect for local cultures, policies, or economies. Given that the arrival of Catholicism in Japan was also concurrent with advances in gunnery, some warlords aligned themselves with the West not just because of an interest in personal regeneration or religious conviction, but purely for political and military motivations.

By the end of the nineteenth century, the Tokugawa regime was losing its hold on power. The population was growing increasingly dissatisfied with the government, and many blamed the Shogun. In addition, Buddhist priests were the cause of dissatisfaction due to corruption and moral decay among them. The population distrusted them and felt certain apathy toward Buddhism.

Since the Emperor played no political role during the Tokugawa Period, the Japanese people began to look to him as a moral authority. Due to the Shogun's unpopularity, the Shogun eventually relinquished power in 1867 and the Tokugawa Period officially ended. In 1867, a new Emperor came to power and ruled Japan until 1912. This is called the Meiji Period — a time of modernization.

As mentioned in chapter two, prior to 1867, under the leadership of Commodore Matthew Galbraith Perry, missionaries had arrived in Japan (1853) to force the long-secluded country to open its doors to the outside world. The message Perry brought to Japan's leaders from President Millard Fillmore was forward looking in very general terms. It led to the establishment of mutually beneficial trade relations. Although on the surface, Perry's demands seemed relatively modest, according to John W. Dower, for Americans, this was but one momentous step in a seemingly inexorable process of westward expansion. They ultimately spilled across the Pacific to embrace the exotic "East." For the Japanese, on the other hand, the intrusion of Perry's warships was traumatic, confounding, fascinating, and ultimately devastating.[5]

The opening of Japan to the West, especially to the Americans, meant the discovery of new frontiers across the Pacific Ocean. The markets and heathen souls of "Asia" — steeped in myth and mystery —beckoned more enticingly than ever before. Mars, Mammon, and God ventured there hand-in-hand in this dawning age of technological advancement and commercial revolution.[6]

7.1.1 State Shinto

The opening of Japan to the West did not, in and of itself, mean that the country was receptive to Christianity. As outlined in chapter two, Christianity was initially unwelcome and only later did Western pressure force Japan to ease its policies toward Christianity. However, the decision to allow it to re-enter Japan, together with the nation's past experience with missionaries, triggered a serious political and religious reaction. At this time State Shinto was created as an alternative to Christianity and it gradually was integrated within Japanese politics. John Breen argues that:

The fear offers a persuasive, if ultimately partial, explanation for the early Meiji enthusiasm for Shinto in all of its various aspects. They cite evidence that the development of new state rituals and local shrine rites, the articulation of shrine policies and the creation of a national shrine network, the promotion of Shinto funerals and the establishment of shrine registration, not to mention the different Shinto theological formulations produced and disseminated in turn by the Jingikan[7] and, following its failure in 1871, the Kyobusho, were all linked to government paranoia about the Christian threat.[8]

In 1868, Meiji authorities established a government office called the Shinto Worship Bureau. It served to control religious activities and ensure the separation of Buddhism from Shinto. Some believe that the establishment of State Shinto and the deification of the Emperor amounted to the creation of an alternative to Christianity: Jesus is both King and God, and this ensures the loyalty of His followers. Thus, in the State Shinto a similar concept *(Tenno)*, i.e. the Emperor who is god incarnate, is an alternative to belief in Christ. As a god *(kami)*, the Emperor was eternal, pure, inviolable and sacred; the divine channel for blessing and nurture from the ancestral gods to their descendants.[9]

In 1871, all of the Shinto shrines in Japan became the property of the government. They were officially ranked and each received government funds for maintenance and functioning. Thus, the *Ise* Shrine at the top of the government list was dedicated to *Amaterasu no Omikami*. State Shinto held that the Imperial family was directly linked to this deity. In 1890, the *Imperial Rescript on Education* was issued, and students were required to ritually recite its vows and affirm their total loyalty to the State — even to the point of death, understood as self-sacrifice. The 1930s saw an intensification of the efforts of the Department of Education to ensure that the pupils at private Christian schools took part in the national rites at State Shinto shrines. The authorities aimed to exclude foreign ideas that might pollute the values of loyalty and patriotism. They were particularly intent on inculcating these into the young.[10]

The new Japanese law forced Christian institutions to obey Japanese authorities and also to participate in the rituals of the national religion. Christians and members of other institutions that refused to co-operate were severely persecuted. Church leaders were forced to pay respect to and honor the Emperor, and even to visit the *Ise* Shrine for rituals and pledge contributions to the nation's well-being and interest. Of course, these kinds of rituals did not accord with Christian doctrine. The Japanese government even required that nationalistic sermons be preached in the churches. This forced participation of Christians in state-sponsored Shinto ceremonies, the "shrine question," touched a sensitive nerve for Christians as it called into question their loyalty, patriotism, and attitude toward the Emperor.[11] Participating in State Shinto rites was troublesome because it was unclear whether or not it constituted a religious act.[12]

In the late 1930s, religions, including Christianity, were asked to participate in a spiritual mobilization campaign. Ion argues that some Christians saw this as an opportunity to show their solidarity with this campaign by enthusiastically endorsing the government's call for a new order in East Asia via the expansion of missionary work in Manchuria and north China. This was to follow Japan's military advance into those areas. At this moment, Japanese Christians felt that they had a responsibility to undertake evangelistic work on the Asian continent.[13]

Japan's Imperial Constitution openly confirmed the privileged position of State Shinto, but it also guaranteed freedom of religion as long as the government approved doctrines and rituals. This meant that the government nationalized every existing religion, including Christianity. Thus, it was forcibly placed under the umbrella organization of *Nippon Kirisuto Kyodan, (Kyodan).*

Japanese Christianity in the pre-1945 period was a strong force within the intellectual groups of the Christian movement. It provided a theological rationale for Christians who wanted to harmonize the goals of their movement with those of the state. Japanese Christianity went so far in this that some groups associated with it advocated what is termed Imperial Way Christianity *(Kodo Krisutokyo),* [14] a version of government-controlled Christianity that was committed to supporting Japan's expansionist and imperialist ventures.

It was during this time of growing militarism that the charismatic Holiness leader, Juji Nakada (1870–1939), promoted the idea of Japan as a chosen nation. He proposed that, like the

Jewish people, God had chosen the Japanese. His nationalistic interpretation of the Bible was fostered by the revival, but, in 1933, it led to serious doctrinal conflicts between Holiness leaders.[15]

7.2 Capitulation

After the defeat of Japan by the Allied Forces in 1945, the Shinto State was dismantled and the practice of worshipping the Emperor abolished. Religious freedom was granted to all groups, including Christians. However, the American government endorsed Christianity in Japan and encouraged missionaries to travel to post-war Japan in an effort to evangelize the nation. By 1946, many *Kyodan* churches had returned to their old denominational structures and taken their old names. Hence, the so-called unity that had been brought about by force was abolished. In what follows, I discuss the implications of Japan's capitulation and the impact this had on Christianity in there.

7.2.1 The Atomic Bombs

Japan's growing power and the atrocities committed by her military during World War II, together with the attack on Pearl Harbor, gave the Americans justification to attack Hiroshima and Nagasaki with atomic bombs. These had been invented by the United States and were being tested for the first time on Japan. This ended the war in 1945 and resulted in Japan's surrender. According to Mark Selden:

> From the earliest reports of the atomic bombings,
> Americans have viewed nuclear destruction primarily
> from the Promethean perspective of the inventor and

bombardier. The carefully crafted image of a mushroom cloud spiraling heavenward has represented to most Americans the bomb as the ultimate symbol of victory in a 'Good War' that carried the United States to the peak of its power and prosperity. In this story, Americans were portrayed as a brave, selfless, and united people who responded to treachery with total mobilization culminating in a knockout victory.[16]

On August 9, 1945, the second of two atomic bombs — the only two ever used as instruments of aggression against essentially defenseless civilian populations — was dropped on Nagasaki. It devastated the oldest center of Christianity in the country.[17] As Gary G. Kohls notes, not only was Nagasaki the site of the largest Christian church in the Orient, St. Mary's Cathedral, but it also had the largest concentration of baptized Christians in all of Japan.[18] This can only have further complicated the Japanese view of Christianity: How could the West, which "represented" Christianity, destroy a city that had such a rich history of Christian culture and a large Christian population?

7.2.2 Surrender

The bombing of Hiroshima and Nagasaki led the Japanese government to surrender to the Allies, on August 14, 1945. On August 15, 1945, Emperor Hirohito announced Japan's unconditional surrender in a radio broadcast. Japan of 1945 was an occupied, conquered, and defeated superpower, a fallen imperialist nation. All that remained of

174

it were the ruins of war, chaos, poverty, and disease.

In the summer of 1945, Japan was a nation exhausted both physically and morally as the historian, John W. Hall notes. According to Hall, since the outbreak of the second Sino–Japanese war in 1937, 3.1 million Japanese (of whom 800,000 were civilians) had lost their lives. Over 30 percent of Japanese people had lost their homes. [19] There was a food shortage and the transportation system was barely functioning. Acute food shortages had reduced much of the country to near starvation. Civilian morality broke down as farmers reaped tremendous profits by selling food on the black market. Wealthy families bartered heirlooms for the necessities of life.[20] The nation's industry had been smashed, reduced to one quarter of its previous capacity and the country was on the verge of inflation. The people were also emotionally and intellectually bewildered after having been fed with exaggerated wartime propaganda and hyper-nationalist values over a period of several years. All of this propaganda lost its force with Japan's unconditional surrender.[21]

Japan fell under the supervision of the Supreme Commander of Allied Powers (SCAP) under the leadership of General Douglas MacArthur. SCAP's policy required that the country go through three major phases: demilitarization, democratization, and rehabilitation. In short, the Japan of World War II was to be totally dismantled. Certain laws that had been imposed in the Meiji Period were rescinded. Also, the notion of the divinity of the Japanese emperor was abolished. Democratic laws were promulgated and political parties came to play a key role in the political scene.

175

7.2.3 The Emperor, MacArthur and Christianity

In his message of surrender, Emperor Hirohito (1901–1989) stated, "Moreover, the enemy has begun to employ a new and most cruel bomb, the power of which to do damage is, indeed, incalculable, taking the toll of many innocent lives. Should we continue to fight, not only would it result in an ultimate collapse and obliteration of the Japanese nation, but also it would lead to the total extinction of human civilization."[22] He declared that the military would be disarmed and suggested that this was not because disarmament had been forced upon Japan, but because the country had made the difficult choice to favor peace.[23] Despite the surrender of Japan, Emperor Hirohito spoke of the United States as an enemy, even though he had a choice not to do so. Can it be that through the early years after the occupation, people therefore would see America as their enemy and Christianity as the enemy's religion? In his blog, Rob Kerby, senior editor of Beliefnet writes that the Allied Supreme Commander, Douglas MacArthur thought Japan needed Jesus. He argues that in the late 1940s and throughout the 1950s, MacArthur freely described post-war Japan as existing in a spiritual vacuum. MacArthur argued that all their gods had failed them — Japan's invincible military, its divine emperor, and its 1,000-year belief that the Land of the Rising Sun would rule the world. Now the conquered people of Japan had nothing.[24]

Kerby further indicates that, in 1955, MacArthur told *U.S. News and World Report*, that no phase of the occupation had left him with a greater sense of personal satisfaction than his spiritual stewardship of the country. Thus, as I mentioned in chapter five, over the next five years, more than 5,000 missionaries from various churches and mission organizations went to Japan and flooded the nation with millions of Bibles.[25]

In his book *Unconditional Democracy: Education and Politics in Occupied Japan 1945-1952,* Toshio Nishi argues that MacArthur saw himself as both savior and Caesar. In his book Nishi quotes MacArthur's own words: "I could make the Emperor and seventy million people Christian overnight, if I wanted to use the power I have."[26] According to Nishi, MacArthur's faith in Christianity had become his political doctrine: Christianity equaled democracy.[27] Nishi writes:

> To MacArthur, the Japanese surrender signified something more than mere military defeat. It symbolized "the collapse of a faith," that "left a complete vacuum morally, mentally, and physically. And into this vacuum flowed the democratic way of life . . . The moral vacuum that MacArthur perceived in Japanese soul was to be filled by a specific theological doctrine. Christianity, he believed, was imbued with "spiritual repugnance of war." He therefore tried to create in defeated Japan "a complete spiritual reformation," effective not only now but for generations to come, that would conduct the Japanese people "from feudalistic slavery to human freedom, from the immaturity that comes from mythical teachings and legendary ritualism to

177

maturity of enlightened knowledge and truth, from blind fatalism of war to the considered realism . . . Japan was therefore "the world's great laboratory for an experiment" in which "a race, long stunted by ancient concepts of mythological teaching," could be uplifted by "practical demonstrations of Christian ideals."[28]

In a *Japan Times* article, Mikio Haruna indicates that MacArthur pondered to convince Emperor Hirohito to convert to Christianity. Haruna argues "MacArthur's idea of spreading Christianity in Japan by having the Emperor change his religion probably stemmed from the general's belief that democracy arises from Christian principles."[29] According to Ray Moore, professor of Japanese history at Amherst College in Massachusetts, MacArthur told an American audience that he was "a soldier of God as well as of the republic." In October 1945, MacArthur urged Protestant leaders in the United States to send a "thousand missionaries" to try to convert Japan to Christianity.[30]

In November 1945, the Emperor, met with a group of Protestant leaders, and, in 1946, with Catholic leaders. At that time, it was apparently believed that if the Emperor were to convert from Shinto to Christianity, many ordinary Japanese would follow suit.[31] Such meetings gave rise to a rumor that the Emperor would indeed do this. In an August 1948 interview with Australia's *Melbourne Sun* newspaper, the Emperor himself denied the rumor that he wanted to become a Christian. He told the paper that it would be better for him to retain his Shinto beliefs. However, the *Imperial Rescript* was issued on New Year's Day of 1946, by which the Emperor denied that he had divine character as a man-god *(ara-hito kami).* Hideo Kishimoto suggests that Brigadier General Dyke and Premier Kijuro Shidehara had decided the contents of the rescript.[32]

Kishimoto rightfully argues that this action put an end to totalitarian State Shinto, for the concept of the Emperor as a man-god had been misused not only for the suppression of religions but also to restrict religious faith.[33] He considered strengthening his contacts with Christians for a certain period of time and showing an interest in Western civilization—all in an effort to protect the Imperial system.[34]

Kishida writes that the Japanese did not fight the war either in self-defense or for national gain; they also did not seek to liberate Asian nations from Western domination. They fought in order to protect their pride and avoid humiliation.[35] However, the Japan's surrender in 1945, placed her under obvious foreign control, and so government leaders decided they should try a second type of self-deception, namely, denying the reality of this humiliation itself.[36] Kishida writes:

> If we look at the ways the Japanese have dealt with state of humiliation, we see a clear difference between the means taken by the Meiji leaders and what was done after the defeat in the Pacific War. The leaders of the Meiji government appealed to the world at every opportunity they had, insisting that the

treaties Japan had to sign with the United States and
the Western nations were unequal and humiliating.
They expected a great deal of effort trying to abolish
them. The Japan-US Mutual Security Treaty, signed
in 1951, on the other hand, has never been defined
as unequal; not only has the Japanese government
made little attempt to abolish it, but Japan appears
to want to keep it forever. [37]

According to Kishida the Japanese government insisted that Japan
and United States were equal partners, and that their relationship
was based on mutual trust and respect.[38] Having experienced
total defeat, they were now firmly resolved not to try to challenge
American control in any way. They were convinced that nothing was
wrong with being under someone else's defensive umbrella. Such
people according to Kishida wanted to retain some shred of belief in
Japanese autonomy in a Japan that makes all of its decisions on its
own and is only subject to American influence.[39]

In the eyes of the victor, the surrender of Japan was
triumphant and glorious; from the perspective of the defeated
nation, it was extraordinarily humiliating. Japanese culture does not
condone expressing one's feelings directly; only indirect expression
is acceptable. Doing the former can cause humiliation. Defeat of a
political system is understandable, but imposing one's religion upon
a nation, especially upon her Emperor can bring the highest level
of disgrace. First of all, "forcing" an Emperor to deny his divinity
and then asking him to become a Christian does not make a good

impression. From a Japanese perspective, it evidences a high level of arrogance.

7.2.4 Democracy and Religion

One of the important aims of SCAP was to implement a Western model of democracy; it sought to enforce separation of state and religion, especially separation of State Shinto from the state. America advocated and implemented a Shinto-free state given the relationship that had developed between State Shinto and Japan's imperial power and the way in which it had driven the nation's ambitions. On December 15, 1945, in order to separate State Shinto from the state and thereby weaken it, SCAP issued a memorandum to the Japanese Government entitled "Abolition of Government Sponsorship, Support, Perpetuation, Control and Dissemination of State Shinto (*Kottka Shinto, Jinja Shinto*). This is popularly called the Shinto Directive.[40] Kishimoto writes:

> Through this directive SCAP forbade the state and local public bodies to treat the shrines in any special way, such as giving them financial grants from public funds, or regarding shrine priests as government officials. Other matters prohibited were: the collection of contributions (for shrines, temples, churches, etc.) and the distribution of amulets by public or neighborhood associations, the utilization of public facilities in connection with religious ceremonies and festivals, the placing of small Shinto

altars *(kamidana)* in government offices or public
schools, the conduct of ceremonies to purify building
sites and celebrate the completion of the framework
of public buildings, the conduct of, or participation
in ceremonies to give notice of the assumption of a
new position on the part of government and public
officials in their official capacity, teaching of Shinto
doctrine in public schools, and sponsoring visits and
worship at shrines in groups under the leadership of
a teacher.[41]

Moreover, the Directive stated: "Shrine Shinto (State Shinto), after
having been divorced from the State and divested of its militaristic
and ultra-nationalistic elements, will be granted the same protection
as any other religion in so far as it may in fact be the religion or a
philosophy of Japanese individuals."[42]

According to Tsuneki Noguchi, the separation of state and
religion in Japan is fundamentally unthinkable. He believes that in
Japan, throughout history, religion and politics have been united for
a long time. Noguchi ironically believes that, during the occupation
period, the separation of Shinto from the state was similar to putting
birds in the water and make fishes live on the land.[43] It amounted to
doing violence to the culture and is, in the Japanese mind, extremely
irrational and a problem of life or death for the country.[44] Noguchi
believes that when the *Shinto Directive* spoke about the separation
of religion and state (not of church and state as is the case in
modern European history), this was an attempt to sever not only the

shrines but all Shinto elements from the state, and so to eradicate the very spiritual foundations of the nation. The purpose of this directive is to put all religions, faiths, and creeds upon exactly the same legal basis and to forbid their affiliation with the government.[45]

The question that remains is how impartial this initiative of separation of state and religion actually was. The very fact that MacArthur, the supreme commander of the allied forces, preferred to impose Christianity on a Japanese emperor as well as on the Japanese people, raises a lot of questions among many Japanese as to whether this separation of state and religion was genuine and carried out impartially.

On the other hand, as we know, there is no doubt that State Shinto contributed greatly to Japan's imperialistic ambitions. The question may therefore be asked, if only silently by the Japanese, whether Western Christianity is as clean as State Shinto when it comes to war crimes throughout history. For example, according to Kishida, the United States is a country built upon, and expanded by, killing and stripping native inhabitants of their pride and land. In order for the nation to survive such a troubled history, it had to behave callously. Kishida argues that this blindness and insensitivity has caused the United States to provoke unnecessary conflicts throughout the world, even in Japan.[46]

According to Hiroshi Suzuki, the primary reason why Japanese react negatively to Christianity is the darker aspect of the history of the Western world.[47] Suzuki proposes that the Japanese relate to the tragic life of Jesus, but not to the history of the West, where Christianity is predominant.[48] They respond negatively when

183

they see atrocities committed by Westerners against other Asians or Africans, or in their own society. In their view, a religion that cannot change the moral quality of a society cannot be a good one.[49] In his paper, Suzuki raises questions concerning the tragic 9/11 attacks. He more or less criticizes America's intervention in Afghanistan and indirectly compares American reaction to 9/11 to the American response to Pearl Harbor in 1945.[50]

The second important fact that calls into question the democracy imposed on Japan is the censorship carried out by the SCAP authorities during the Occupation Period (1945–1952). Monica Braw, senior researcher at the European Institute of Japanese Studies, Stockholm School of Economics has done an extensive research on censorship during the period of the occupation. She writes:

> Like in war, in SCAP headquarters there was an Intelligence Section. To this was added a Civil Intelligence Section with a Civil Censorship Detachment and a Press, Pictorial and Broadcast Division. Here, censorship of Japanese newspapers, radio and books was undertaken. Many Koreans and Taiwanese, who knew both Japanese and English, were used as censors because there were not many American soldiers who knew Japanese. Some Nisei and some Japanese, who had kept up their English during the war by themselves, also worked as censors. One of the first censorship punishments

meted out concerned the atomic bomb. The news
agency Domei, which nowadays is called Kyodo,
was prohibited to continue broadcasting abroad in
September 1945.[51]

Braw observes that, on September 14, 1945, Domei News Agency
was punished and closed down for 24 hours. It was accused of
having disturbed public tranquility by using the sentence: "Japan
might have won the war but for the atomic bomb, a weapon too
terrible to face and one which only barbarians would use." On
September 18, Asahi Newspaper was closed down for two days for
having quoted Hatoyama Ichiro, who later became prime minister.
He called the use of the atomic bomb a war crime which violated
international law and said: "So long as the United States advocates
'might is right', it cannot deny that the use of the atomic bomb and
the killing of innocent people is a violation of international law and
a war crime worse than an attack on a hospital ship or the use of
poison gas."[52]

If SCAP was there to promote democracy, then why did it
violate one of the most fundamental principles of democracy; the
right of a free press, in early post-world War II Japan? Of course, from
the perspective of the winner, it was indeed necessary to bring order
to Japan. Still, what would a Japanese person think when it comes
to this? Could it be that some of the Japanese people consider this
as a double standard? Can censorship of basic opinions ever be in
alignment with the fundamentals of democracy?

7.3 War Guilt Information Program

SCAP also organized the *War Guilt Information Program*. It aimed to implant a sense of war guilt in the minds of Japanese through "education." If it were to be successful, the resulting sense of war guilt would be passed on to future generations.

On September 5, 1946, the first official post-war Japanese history textbook appeared under the title of *Kuni no Ayumi* (The Progress of the Country). In advance Japanese historians had been ordered to write textbooks that were not propagandist. They could not advocate militarism, ultra-nationalism or Shinto doctrine and had to avoid descriptions of Emperors simply because they were Emperors.[53] The *War Guilt Information Program* was expanded to include procedural measures against Japanese attitudes toward the bombing of Hiroshima and Nagasaki, as well as ultra-nationalistic advertising during the Tokyo War Tribunal.[54]

On October 22, 1945 SCAP instructed the Japanese government to immediately re-appoint teachers and educational officials who had been dismissed or forced to resign for holding liberal or anti-militaristic opinions or conducting such activities during the War. In addition, under the supervision of SCAP, all militaristic and nationalistic personnel were removed from the educational system.

In his paper, "Some Aspects of Humanism that Combines East and West: MacArthur, Showa Tenno, and Justice Pal" Tomosaburo Yamauchi speaks about the cultural imperialism demonstrated by the United States of America. Yamauchi quotes the words of John Whitney Hall (1916–1997), son of an American missionary born in Tokyo and a prominent pioneer in Japanese Studies:

186

We (the United States) have all too easily taken the
role of the protector of "Civilization", equating our
private national interests with the higher aims of
history. The sense of moral superiority (which was the
certitude of our missionaries) and of technological
superiority (which is our national faith) combine in
our minds to give a particular aura of inevitability to
our action in Asia. The Occupation was too easy a
chance "to realize the ethnocentric American sense
of mission" to remake our enemy in our image. And
unhappily for us, Japanese behavior in the postwar
years only reinforced our predilection to play the "big
brother". Japan has our approval so long as it plays
our game and minds its own business.[55]

He also argues that MacArthur, the Christian general, freely
delivered 10,000,000 copies of the Bible to the Japanese public.
He articulated his goal for the occupation was stated publicly, in
a speech in which he stressed the need to correct the traditional
social order under which the Japanese people have been living for
centuries.[56] Thus, the Christian mission of Occupation Period was
also conducted in the context of the *War Guilt Information Program*.

John H. Minagawa wrote in the Newsletter *Pray For This
Nation* (11 May, 2003) that the *War Guilt Information Program* was to
implant the guilty feeling that the Greater East Asian War was a war
of aggression to the Japanese, they thoroughly disseminated the
information through the mass communications such as newspapers,

magazines, radio broadcast, etc." He further argues that the biased public education by the leftist ideology have taught the Japanese history as "the history of aggressions against Asian nations by the Imperial militarism" for the past 50 years after the war.[57]

Yukio Tanaka remembers the tragic event of September 11, 2001 and expresses his sorrow about this tragedy, but he also asks "Why?" He responds by suggesting that the American national psyche cannot but repeat the same pattern of aggressive action in dealing with the "other." This will, however, not cease so long as rationalization (i.e., justifying military action) and illusion (a self-image that America is the "just" nation) continue to dominate the American public consciousness.[58]

7.4 The Yasukuni Shrine

As mentioned earlier, in 1868 the Emperor's position was restored to that of a living-god and he was recognized as the direct descendent of the Sun Goddess. It was at this point that Shinto became the state religion. With the revival of Shinto during the Meiji Period, new shrines were created to promote the idea of loyalty to the Emperor. Thus, the *Yasukuni* shrine, initially called Tokyo *Shokonsha* (Tokyo Spirit-Inviting Shrine), was established in 1869 for the purpose of honoring political leaders and samurai who opposed the shogunate's policy of opening the country to the West.[59] The idea behind such a monument was that, when a Japanese person died in the service of the Emperor, his spirit would be enshrined within its walls. Upon his first visit there in 1874, the Emperor composed a poem; "I assure those of you who fought and died for your country

that your names will live forever at this shrine in Musashino."[60] In
1879, Tokyo *Shokonsha*'s name was changed to *Yasukuni Jinja* (the
Shrine to Ease the Nation).

Over the years, *Yasukuni's* role changed so that dying for the
Emperor was synonymous with dying for Japan. It would continue
to fulfill this role until the end of World War II. According to the
officials of the *Yasukuni* Shrine, it is not only soldiers' spirits that are
enshrined here, but also those of other people:

> "There are women and school girls divinities who
> were involved in relief operations on the battlefields,
> a great number of students who went to work in
> factories for the war effort. There also enshrined
> ordinary Japanese citizens, Taiwanese and Korean
> people who died as Japanese, people who died
> during the Siberian detention   having been labeled
> war criminals, tried by the Allies and executed.
> Here at Yasukuni Shrine, these people, regardless
> of their rank or social standing, are considered to
> be deserving of completely equal respect and
> worship because the only purpose of the shrine is to
> commemorate those who sacrificed their lives for their
> nation. That is, the 2,466,000 divinities enshrined
> at Yasukuni Shrine all represent individuals who
> sacrificed their lives to the public duty of protecting
> their motherland."[61]

189

After World War II, *Yasukuni* shrine became one of the most controversial political and religious topics in Japan; for the former Japanese colonies in Asia, it represents a symbol of Japanese militarism and aggression and is viewed to exist only for the purpose of glorifying the war.[62] Others who oppose the prime ministers official visit to the *Yasukuni* Shrine argue that official recognition of it amounts to the revival of the State Shinto[63], which was banned by the occupation force as discussed previously.

As the criticisms make clear, the Japanese representatives official visit to *Yasukuni* was and is problematic. It is claimed, for example, that the Japanese prime minister should not visit on the *Yasukuni* Shrine officially because of: 1) the military perspective it entails, 2) government support of the *Yasukuni* shrine re-creates an unbreakable link between Shintoism and the political administration which created the State Shinto, 3) official recognition of the *Yasukuni* means that the government supports the institution which promoted Japanese aggression in Asia.[64]

As soon as the foreign occupation ended with the signing of peace treaty on September 8, 1951, the Autumn Festival was observed and for the first time after the war, Prime Minister Yoshida paid his respects to the *Yasukuni* Shrine. The following year the Emperor, who had become the symbolic head of the country, followed suit.[65] In relation to such visits, a piece of proposed legislation was designed to allow state support for *Yasukuni* shrine and repeatedly introduced in the Diet. This bill represented a return to the wartime relationship of *Yasukuni* with the State.[66] Supported by the Association of Bereaved Families *(izokukai),* its aim was to change

190

the status of *Yasukuni* from that of a religious, juridical individual to a state-sponsored 'special purpose religious corporation.'[67] *Izokukai* is said to be an influential organization, not only with respect to the *Yasukuni* Shrine, but also in political circles.[68] However, the bill was defeated four times between 1969 and 1974 and also a fifth time in 1974 when the Liberal Democratic Party (LDP), introduced it to the House of Representatives.[69] One of the reasons why it failed to pass the legislature was the pressure applied by the religious world, especially the Christian churches and some new Buddhist religious organizations. Both conducted an energetic campaign against it. [70]

Christian churches, especially National Christian Council in Japan have regularly opposed the visits of Japanese officials and prime ministers *Yasukuni* shrine. For instance, in September 25, 2006, a statement letter from National Christian Council in Japan was directed to Japan's Prime Minister. It called for Japan to admit the wrongs of aggressive warfare and to embrace the principles of the Japanese Constitution:

> "We Christians are taught that "Justice exalts a nation, but sin is a reproach to all people." However, in the past we were witness to the sins of our nation as it pursued aggressive warfare and colonialist policies in other Asian nations. We did not protest, but in fact committed the sin of accepting and supporting these policies. Repenting of these sins, we have strived through prayer, verbal protest and action, to call our nation to admit the wrongs of aggressive warfare

191

and colonialist policies, and to stand firmly on the principles of peaceful non-aggression, the sovereignty of the people, and respect for basic human rights as clearly stated in the Japanese Constitution.

However, Prime Minister Koizumi, you have trampled on our desires, and since August 13, 2001, have continued obstinately to push ahead with yearly visits to worship at Yasukuni Shrine culminating in the visit this year on August 15. We rigorously protest these visits to worship at the Yasukuni Shrine by the Prime Minister of Japan. The Prime Minister, as representative of the Japanese people, is infringing on Article 20 of the Japanese Constitution when he makes an official visit to worship at Yasukuni Shrine. Such visits were deemed unconstitutional by a judgment put forth by the Osaka High Court on September 30, 2005. This is not a matter of criticism from our Asian neighbors. The Prime Minister ought to conform to the law and Constitution of Japan. Ever since 1969 when the Liberal Democratic Party submitted the Yasukuni Shrine Bill, we the people have continued to protest any connection between the Yasukuni Shrine and the nation state. We strongly urge that the head of state lend an ear to the voices of the people, and terminate any visits to Yasukuni Shrine . . . "[71]

This letter made it evident that Christians in Japan have continually opposed Japanese officials' visiting the *Yasukuni* shrine and it indicates that they have repented from the past sins committed by the Japanese against other nations in Asia. Public opposition to this, especially that carried out by Christian organizations, may influence the image of Christianity among the general public for several reasons: first of all, as indicated in chapter three, the Japanese culture is one of silence. One is expected to withhold one's opinion in public, even when it is justified and correct.

Secondly, Christian churches, in so far as they constantly oppose the war shrine visits on principle, may be giving a mixed signal to the Japanese people. They might think that their statements and objections are politically motivated, in particular, that their objections are inspired by the West and so rooted in the problematic relationship of which Japanese Christianity has with the West.

Further, according to Mike Rogers, the author of *Schizophrenic in Japan: An American Ex-Pat's Guide to Japanese and American Society/Politics & Humor* (2005):

> "This is an important part of the misunderstanding about Yasukuni Shrine. The shrine is in no way financed by the State. It is illegal for the State to make any financial donations to Yasukuni Shrine. The Prime Minister — as an individual — and just like the President of the United States—has the right to visit any church of his choice.

The Japanese thinking on this matter goes like this: the current constitution of Japan, written by the US Occupation Authority, requires a separation of religion and politics, but the United States itself does not follow those rules. Doesn't the US President put his hand on the bible to take an oath of office at inauguration? Is it not impossible to rid any country of some form of religious rites in public and private ceremonies? This is why the Japanese don't understand why China, South Korea, and North Korea make such a big deal out of some elected official visiting a shrine."[72]

On the other hand, since *Yasukuni* enshrines the dead and even war criminals, visiting the *Yasukuni* shrine may have powerful cultural implications. As indicated in chapter four, the Japanese have a special way of treating their deceased and their ancestors. They have rituals and duties which they must perform in relation to their dead. Regardless who the ancestor was, a holy man, an ordinary man or a criminal, one's ancestor will always remain an ancestor and those who are living have the duty to performing rites and show their respect towards them.

In chapter four I indicated that, in the Japanese context, sin (i.e., crime) is forgiven when one acknowledges it and either asks for forgiveness or pays the necessary price (i.e. imprisonment, death penalty etc.). Thus, according to Rogers, "since all convicted Japanese war criminals were either executed or sentenced to life in

194

prison, they paid their penalty — as prescribed by the Allied victors of the war — and then the souls of the dead were "cleansed" by the ritual at *Yasukuni* Shrine as was the case with all who died in Japan's wars."[73] Furthermore and in this same context, some Japanese may believe that Japan collectively was punished by the allied forces when the nuclear bombs were dropped on Japan, so they may not understand the controversy around this issue reflected in media by the Christian groups, especially those linked with Korea and United States. On the other hand, from the perspective of the victims of the war, it is indeed painful to witness the Japanese state officials remembering war criminals by paying a visit to *Yasukuni* Shrine.

Despite all of the opinions concerning the *War Guilt Program* in Japan, or the controversies surrounding the *Yasukuni* Shrine, the fact remains that both the West and Japan have indeed committed crimes against humanity. The question that naturally arises is whether one crime can be justified over against another? Or, is history primarily shaped and written by the victors? Exactly what role should Western Christianity play here? Should American allies in Asia who have been victims of Japanese aggression, especially Christians in South Korea, Taiwan or China, constantly demand apologies from the Japanese people or its government? Does public expression of such opinions have a negative influence on the way Japanese view Christianity?

Based on what has been discussed throughout this chapter, I now distinguish three phases in the development of the Japanese view of Christianity related to political factors:

1. By the end of sixteenth century, Christianity was viewed as the religion of Western intruders who intended to Christianize Japan as they did in other parts of the world.

2. During the Meiji Period and until the end of World War II, Japanese authorities considered Western Christianity to be a rival to their own religion. During this same period, Japan became the strongest non-Western rival to the Western nations where imperialism was concerned. It successfully competed with the West in many areas, namely militarily, technologically and scientifically.

3. After World War II, during the early years of the occupation, Japan might have taken Western Christianity to be the religion of the occupiers. Thus, one of the factors why Christianity succeeded in South Korea was because it was seen as the religion of the liberator (i.e., United States). In Japan, it was likely viewed as the religion of the enemy. Martien Brinkman writes:

> Religion in Japan, including Christianity, is linked very emphatically with recent state history. This complicates the position of the churches, which is probably also one of the reasons for

the fact that Christianity has spread widely in Korea but not in Japan. In Korea, Christianity was quickly viewed as an important ideological power over against Japanese colonization. For Koreans, identification with Christianity became means for fighting for their national identity over the Japanese occupation. Christianity brought over American missionaries was just what was needed in Korea in the beginning of the twentieth century. The missionaries had nothing to do with this aspect, it was the Koreans themselves who allotted Christianity this role.[74]

Finally, as the content of this chapter makes clear, political factors do indeed play a role in the unsuccessful, or marginally successful, reception of Christianity in Japan. Here, it can be safely generalized that it is the Japanese view of Christianity, namely as the religion of the West, has been influenced by the sort of political developments cited above.

Notes

1   Mullins, "The Social and Legal Status of Religious Minorities in Japan" (paper presented at International Coalition for Religious Freedom Conference on "Religious Freedom and the New Millennium," Tokyo, May 23–25, 1998).

2   Ibid.

3   Ibid.

4 Reischauer and Craig, 75.

5 John W. Dower, "Black Ships & Samurai: Commodore Perry and the Opening of Japan (1853-1854)", Visualizing Cultures, http://ocw.mit. edu/ans7870/21f/21f.027/black_ships_and_samurai/bss_ essay02.html

6 Ibid.

7 Department of Divinities also known as the Department of Shinto Affairs

8 John Breen, "Shinto and Christianity a History of Conflict and Compromise," in *Handbook of Christianity in Japan*, ed. Mark R. Mullins (Leiden: Brill, 2003), 256.

9 Lee, 27.

10 Ion, 82.

11 Ibid.

12 Ibid.

13 Ion, 88.

14 Ion, 88.

15 Ikegami Yoshimasa, "Holiness, Pentecostal, and Charismatic Movements in Modern Japan," in *Handbook of Christianity in Japan*, ed. Mark R. Mullins (Leiden: Brill, 2003), 132.

16 Mark Selden, "Commemoration and Silence: Fifty Years of Remembering the Bomb in America and Japan," in *Living with the Bomb: American and Japanese Cultural Conflicts in the Nuclear Age*, ed. Laura Hein and Mark Selden (Armonk, NY: M.E. Sharpe, 1997), 3.

17 Gary G. Kohls, "The Bombing of Nagasaki August 9, 1945: The Untold Story" http://www.lewrockwell.com/orig5/kohls8.html (August 6, 2007).

198

18 Ibid.

19 John Whitney Hall, *Japan: prehistory to modern times*
(Frankfurt am Main: S. Fischer Verlag, 1991), 349.

20 Hall, 350.

21 Ibid.

22 Emperor Hirohito' Speech on 15th August 1945 https://www.
mtholyoke.edu/acad/intrel/hirohito.htm

23 The full text of Emperor Hirohito' Speech on 15th August 1945
is as follows:

"After pondering deeply the general trends of the world
and the actual conditions obtaining in Our Empire today,
We have decided to effect a settlement of the present
situation by resorting to an extraordinary measure. We
have ordered Our Government to communicate to the
Governments of the United States, Great Britain, China and
the Soviet Union that Our Empire accepts the provisions of
their Joint Declaration.

To strive for the common prosperity and happiness
of all nations as well as the security and well-being of Our
subjects is the solemn obligation which has been handed
down by Our Imperial Ancestors and which lies close to Our
heart. Indeed, We declared war on America and Britain out
of Our sincere desire to ensure Japan's self-preservation
and the stabilization of East Asia, it being far from Our
thought either to infringe upon the sovereignty of other
nations or to embark upon territorial aggrandizement. But
now the war has lasted for nearly four years. Despite the
best that has been done by everyone–the gallant fighting
of the military and naval forces, the diligence and assiduity
of Our servants of the State, and the devoted service of
Our one hundred million people–the war situation has
developed not necessarily to Japan's advantage, while the
general trends of the world have all turned against her
interest. Moreover, the enemy has begun to employ a new

and most cruel bomb, the power of which to do damage is, indeed, incalculable, taking the toll of many innocent lives. Should We continue to fight, not only would it result in an ultimate collapse and obliteration of the Japanese nation, but also it would lead to the total extinction of human civilization.

Such being the case, how are We to save the millions of Our subjects, or to atone Ourselves before the hallowed spirits of Our Imperial Ancestors? This is the reason why We have ordered the acceptance of the provisions of the Joint Declaration of the Powers.

We cannot but express the deepest sense of regret to Our Allied nations of East Asia, who have consistently cooperated with the Empire towards the emancipation of East Asia.

The thought of those officers and men as well as others who have fallen in the fields of battle, those who died at their posts of duty, or those who met with untimely death and all their bereaved families, pains Our heart night and day.

The welfare of the wounded and the war-sufferers, and of those who have lost their homes and livelihood, are the objects of Our profound solicitude.

The hardships and sufferings to which Our nation is to be subjected hereafter will be certainly great. We are keenly aware of the inmost feelings of all of you, Our subjects. However, it is according to the dictates of time and fate that We have resolved to pave the way for a grand peace for all the generations to come by enduring the unendurable and suffering what is unsufferable.

Having been able to safeguard and maintain the structure of the Imperial State, We are always with you, Our good and loyal subjects, relying upon your sincerity and integrity.

Beware most strictly of any outbursts of emotion which may engender needless complications, or any fraternal contention and strike which may create confusion, lead you astray and cause you to lose the confidence of the world.

Let the entire nation continue as one family
from generation to generation, ever firm in its faith in the
imperishability of its sacred land, and mindful of its heavy
burden of responsibility, and of the long road before it.
Unite your total strength, to be devoted to construction
for the future. Cultivate the ways of rectitude, foster
nobility of spirit, and work with resolution—so that you
may enhance the innate glory of the Imperial State and
keep pace with the progress of the world.

(Source: https://www.mtholyoke.edu/acad/intrel/
hirohito.htm)

24 Rob Kirby, "Is it a scandal that Gen. MacArthur thought Christianity would help Japan?" *Beliefnet* accessed April 8, 2013, http://blog.beliefnet.com/on_the_front_lines_of_the_culture_wars/2011/06/scandal-general-douglas-macarthur-thought-christianity-would-help-japan.html.

25 Ibid.

26 Toshio Nishi, *Unconditional Democracy: Education and Politics in Occupied Japan, 1945-1952* (Stanford: Hoover Institution Press, 2004), 43. Nishi refers to William P. Woodard, *The Allied Occupation of Japan 1945-1952 and Japanese Religions* (Leiden: E.J. Brill, 1972), 245.

27 Nishi, 45.

28 Nishi, 42.

29 Mikio Haruna, "MacArthur pondered Showa conversion", *Japan Times*, May 4, 2000, accessed April 8, 2013, http://www.japantimes.co.jp/news/2000/05/04/national/macarthur-pondered-showa-conversion/#.UWMkxL9GfjD.

30 Ibid.

31 Ibid.

32 Hideo Kishimoto, "Reminiscences of Religion in Postwar Japan" (Tokyo: Department of Religious Studies, Tokyo University, 1963), 129.

33 Ibid.

34 Haruna, 2013.

35 Kishida, 24.

36 Kishida, 25.

37 Kishida, 25.

38 Kishida, 26.

39 Ibid.

40 Kishimoto, 127.

41 Ibid.

42 Kishimoto, 128.

43 Tsuneki Noguchi, "Religion and Its Relation to Politics in Japan and the United States", 34. Translated from Noguchi Tsuneki (Professor Emeritus of Kogakkan University), "Nichi-Bei ryokoku ni okeru seiji to shukyo to no kankei" in Shinto Shukvo (Journal of Shinto Studies), no. 87 (April 1977), 17-31.

44 Ibid.

45 Noguchi, 29.

46 Kishida, 5.

47 Hiroshi Suzuki. "Why are Japanese Christians so few?" Paper presented as a seminar talk at the staff meeting of International Friendships Incorporation in Columbus, Ohio on June 26, 2002.

48   Ibid.

49   Ibid.

50   Ibid.

51   Monica Braw, "Discovering the Reasons for American Censorship of the Atomic Bomb in Japan" (lecture presented at 60th anniversary of the atomic bombings of Hiroshima and Nagasaki, Hiroshima University), 2005, 12.

52   Braw, 16.

53   Naoko Kato, 45. Kato refers to John Craiger, "Ienaga Saburo and the First Postwar Japanese History Book" in *Dimensions of Contemporary Japan: Education and Schooling in Japan Since 1945* ed. Edward Beauchamp, (New York: Garland Publishing, 1998), 39-54.

54   Kato, 29.

55   Tomosaburo Yamauchi, "Some Aspects of Humanism that Combines East and West: MacArthur, Showa Tenno, and Justice Pal" in *Bulletin of Osaka Kyoiku University*, Vol.61 No.2, 75-89 (February 13, 2013), 78.

56   Ibid.

57   John H. Minagawa, "Intercessors for Japan" in *Pray For This Nation* (Newsletter may 11, 2003), 10. http://www.christ-ch.or.jp/5_torinashi/back_number/2003/2003.05.eng.pdf

58   Kishida, xii.

59   Shinya Masaaki, "The Politico-Religious Dilemma of the Yasukuni Shrine in Religion and Politics in Present Day Japan." In *Politics and Religion Journa*l: Volume IV, nr.1, Spring (2010), 41-55.

60 "Official Website of Yasukuni Shrine" last visited 1 September, 2013. http://www.yasukuni.or.jp/english/about/index.html

61 Ibid.

62 Shizuka Obara, "The Yasukuni Issue: The process of the State Shinto and its contribution to the Yasukuni Shrine" (paper, Decorah: Luther College, December 5, 2001). http://faculty.luther.edu/~kopfg/interesting/shizukaobara.html

63 Ibid.

64 Ibid.

65 Masaaki, 2010.

66 Ibid.

67 Ibid.

68 Ibid.

69 Ibid.

70 Nobuhiko Takizawa, "Religion and the State in Japan," in *Readings on Church and State*, ed. James E. Wood, Jr. (Waco, TX: J. M. Dawson Institute of Church-State Studies, 1989), 365.

71 Statement letter from National Christian Council in Japan to Japan's Prime Minister on September 25, 2006. http://globalministries.org/news/eap/ncc-japan-opposition-statement-o.html

72 Mike Rogers, "Yasukuni Shrine" December 8, 2005. http://www.lewrockwell.com/2005/12/mike-in-tokyo-rogers/the-yasukuni-shrine/

73 Ibid.

74 Brinkman, 104. Brinkman refers to Mark R. Mullins, "Christianity Transplanted: Toward a Sociology of Success and Failure" in M.R. Mullins and R.F. Young, Eds., *Perspectives on Christianity in Korea and Japan: The Gospel and Culture in East Asia* (Lewiston: Edwin

Mellon, 1995),73 and Y.-B. Kim, "A Re-reading of History of
Asian Missiology from Below: A Korean Perspective" in W. Usdorf
and T. Murayama, eds, *Identity and Marginality: Rethinking
Christianity in North East Asia*, Studies in the Intercultural History of
Christianity 121 (Frankfurt: Peter Lang, 2000), 78-86.

Why is **Christianity** Not Widely
Believed in Japan?

Chapter 8

CHRISTIANITY'S CONTRIBUTION TO JAPANESE LIFE

In the previous chapters, I have discussed various factors that I consider to have played an important role in why Christianity is not widely believed in Japan. However, it would not be correct to neglect to mention the positive impact that Christianity has had on Japan. According to Reischauer "the influence of Christianity on modern Japanese society is far greater than the small number of its adherents would suggest. Christians are strongly represented among the best-educated, leading elements in society and have therefore exerted a quite disproportionate influence."[1] In this chapter, I therefore discuss this latter point from several perspectives, by giving a general overview that is not limited to any particular period in Japanese history. The contributions of Christianity fall into four major categories: education, social justice, theology, and intellectual life.

8.1 Contributions in the Field of Education

Thanks to the efforts of missionaries, various schools and universities were established to advance the Christian faith in Japan and, at the same time, to teach science, technology, and foreign languages. During the Meiji Period, the cause of Christian education was strengthened by the opening of institutions such as Aoyama

University, Meiji University, and Toyo Eiwa University.[2] People like Joseph H. Neesima (1843–1890) were able to interest not only Christians, but also non-Christians in working to establish Doshisha University.

Further, Christianity helped to established girl's schools in Japan.[3] Some of Japan's well-known women's colleges have Christian roots. For example, Tokyo Woman's Christian University was found by Inazo Nitobe (1863–1933), and Tsuda College, a private women's college was found by Umeko Tsuda (1864–1929).[4] Throughout the Tokugawa Period, such schools were a rarity — the natural result of the nationally held conviction that education for women was unnecessary and of little value.

During the Meiji Period and later, Christian missionaries observed that there were few opportunities for Japanese women to obtain an education. The national neglect of their education became clear to them and they responded by establishing schools for girls. Their efforts resulted in the building of several schools in different parts of Japan. The girls who have been educated in these Christian schools have demonstrated the good results that women's education can produce.[5]

In 1890, the number of public high schools for girls increased. Government reports in 1903 state that the number of schools for girls had increased to 155 by that point, and that the total number of students enrolled in them was 35,546. All of them were under the direction of 1,094 women teachers.[6] It should never be forgotten that by word and deed, by work and inspiration, the Christian mission provided a strong impetus for the recognition and solution of this

208

problem in Japan. They made it clear that such education was vitally necessary.[7]

According Nishiyama, the good results obtained from educating Japanese girls through the enthusiastic efforts of Christian missionaries brought about two important changes in Japanese society: they produced an unvarying belief in the need for women's education, and they improved woman's position in Japanese society.[8] Those Japanese girls who received an education showed that Japanese women had an undreamed of capacity for companionship and efficiency. Nishiyama argues that the Japanese should therefore fully appreciate the debt Japanese civilization owes to Christian missionaries in the education of girls.[9] Thanks to their past efforts, a large number of Japanese women are now able to receive an education in various fields. Some Japanese women have entered the business world. Women graduates of the Christian girls' schools were infused with new values of human worth, introduced to a new vision of womanhood.

Although the primary goal of the Christian girls' education was evangelistic, with the passage of time these schools developed into excellent academic institutions offering sophisticated curricula. This eventually produced prestigious seats of higher learning in modern Japan.[10]

8.2 Contributions to Social Justice

Japanese Christians also became important pioneers and leaders in the fields of social justice and social welfare. Prominent personalities included Kanzo Uchimura, who criticized Japan's occupation of

Korea[11], and the social and labor rights activist and author, Toyohiko Kagawa (1888–1960).

The Christian contribution to the improvement of social welfare in Japan is widely recognized. Early efforts at social reform, extending medical care to all, and social work were considered to be a natural part of the Roman Catholic and Protestant mission to the country.[12]

8.2.1 Women's Rights

Although the Meiji restoration offered Japanese women a chance to make a new start, it did not actually improve their social position much. They were merely incorporated into the industrialization and modernization processes and used as a source of cheap labor. The transformation from a feudal society into an industrial capitalist one resulted in various changes in attitude and this, in turn, led to riots and strikes. Moreover, these changes in attitude eventually influenced the social position of women and led to the development of various women's movements in Japan. They began as a strong protest against the miserable position of women during the Meiji era.

The very first women's movements in Japan were influenced by Christianity, and they sought to abolish legal prostitution in Japan. The *Women's Temperance Association* in Japan was the counterpart of various Western organizations such as the Women's Christian Temperance Union. One well- known movement in Japan, *Jiyu Minken Undo* or Movement for Freedom and Popular Rights began in the 1880s. Toshiko Kishida (1864–1901) and Hideko Fukuda

(1865–1927) were the central figures in this. [13] Kishida's strong and charismatic speeches inspired many Japanese women. She fought for equal rights on their behalf. Fukuda later joined Kishida and together they began the Popular Rights Movement. As mentioned earlier, another example of a prominent Christian woman in Japan is Umeko Tsuda (1864–1929), a feminist, educator, and pioneer in education for women during the Meiji Period.[14]

Many other movements and various famous personalities, including Akiko Yosano (1878–1942), Raicho Hiratsuka (1886–1971), and socialist Kikue Hiratsuka (1890–1980), promoted the feminist movement in Japan.[15]

8.2.2 Societal Minorities

Missionaries and native Christians have also played significant role in Japanese society by supporting minorities and the poor. During the Meiji Period, many *burakumin* embraced Christianity. Christian churches and missionaries offered support to them and other minorities. Takujyu Yamagami was one of the pioneers of the Catholic movement for the liberation of the buraku people. Born in 1855, he himself was a *buraku* who became a Christian and decided to fight for the rights of his people. The Catholic Church even has a special commission for this, namely, the Japan Catholic Committee for *Buraku* issues.[16]

One of the well-known Christian activists who helped the poor and vulnerable was Toyohiko Kagawa (1888–1960). Kagawa is also known as the "Saint Francis of Japan".[17] He lived long enough throughout pre- and post-World War II to prove himself to be one of most influential Christian figures on the social justice scene in Japan. In 1909, Kagawa moved into a Kobe slum as a Japanese missionary and social worker. His aim was to help the poverty stricken people of that area. Based on his experience there, he published *Researches in the Psychology of the Poor* (1916). In 1921 and 1922 he was arrested for his part in labor activism during strikes. While in prison he wrote the novels *Crossing the Deathline* and *Shooting at the Sun*. The former was a semi-autobiographical depiction of his time among Kobe's destitute. Kagawa organized the Japanese Federation of Labor as well as the National Anti-War League in 1928. He continued to evangelize Japan's poor, to advocate for women's suffrage and call for a peaceful foreign policy. In 1954 and 1955, Kagawa was nominated for the Nobel Peace Prize. He was posthumously awarded the country's second-highest honor, namely, induction in the *Order of the Sacred Treasure.*

8.2.3 Relief Work

When it comes to Christian relief work, one must certainly also mention the support extended to the Japanese society by of thousands of missionaries and native Christians. For example *Operation Japan*[18] writes the following about the homeless people in Sanya and the role of Christian churches there:

> The number of homeless in the nation reached 20,000 by the end of 1999, up 26 percent from six months previous. About 84 percent of that number are concentrated in Tokyo's 23 wards and the cities

of Yokohama, Kawasaki, Nagoya and Osaka. Most conspicuous in increases were Tokyo's 23 wards, where the homeless population increased from 4,300 to 5,800, up 35%. One of the most concentrated areas is the Taito Ward, slum area of Sanya.

The Salvation Army and several churches are seeking to minister to these people. Most visible among those ministering is the Seikawa (Holy River) Christian Evangelical Church in Sanya, under the leadership of Pastor Haruko Morimoto. She has ministered in that area for 29 years, has served over 1.2 million meals, and baptized nearly 3,000 people. The Sanya Church completed a new large chapel in 1998 which includes lodging facilities for some of the homeless. Pastor Morimoto has become well known throughout Japan for her unique ministry of love and confrontation. Her loud shouts of "Hallelujah!" continue to encourage many who have little hope for rescue.[19]

Both in the past, during the post-World War II era, and in the present after the recent earthquake and tsunami of March 2011, Christians, both individuals and organizations, have been visibly active. Christian relief services provide medical care, shelter, food supplies and moral support.

Over the years, The Japan Evangelical Association's (JEA) Relief and Development Commission has been active in calamity-

213

stricken areas and so provided a good testimony for the evangelical churches. CRASH Japan (Christian Relief, Assistance, Support, and Hope) is a non-profit Christian disaster relief organization based in Tokyo; it is officially recognized by the Japanese government. Before a disaster strikes, they equip and prepare churches and missions so that they can respond effectively. When disaster does strike, CRASH mobilizes Christian volunteers to work with churches and other local ministries. The organization Samaritan's Purse, along with other relief ministries like CRASH and World Vision, has done an outstanding job with its ministry in Japan. The disaster relief in Tohoku after the earthquake and tsunami on March 11 is a case in point.[20]

8.3 Contributions to Christian Theology

In his book, *Japanese Contributions to Christian Theology* (1960), Carl Michelson proposed that, even though Protestant Christianity was relatively young in Japan, this country was apparently the first one to develop its own significant theology.[21] Japan has had many theologians, among them Sato Shigehiko (1887–1935), Seigo Yamaya (1889–1982), Setsuji Otsuka (1887–1977), and Tokutaro Takakura (1885–1934); most of them were mentored by Masahisa Uemura (1857-1925).[22] Takakura's *Evangelical Christianity,* first published in 1924, became a bestseller. He was a disciple of Uemura and continued his mentor's legacy and propagated his theological views.[23] Takakura introduced Evangelicalism with a German flavor and he is known as the man who introduced Calvinism to Japan. Takakura believed that Catholicism, Liberalism, and cultural Christianity were influenced by pagan elements and thus did not represent pure Christianity. He thus opposed liberalism and humanism that he saw "sneaking" into the Christian message.[24]

Shigehiko Sato introduced Luther to Japanese Christians.[25] Leaders such as Shigeru Nakajima (1888–1946), Yonetaru Kimura (1889–1949), and Enkichi Kan (1895–1972) influenced the Social Christianity movement.[26] Nakajima founded the National Alliance for Social Christianity in 1933. He emphasized the difference between community and associations/organizations. Churches and labor unions are examples of associations since they have sets of rules and regulations.[27] He argued that associations are based on sets of rules, but communities are based on personal relationships and only love causes the community to grow. The emphasis was on doing good and helping the poor and the suffering. Despite the fact that it was called Social Christianity, the movement strongly opposed Marxism.[28] It had its own unique ideologies, with Christ as an abstract concept for the concrete process of socialization, a process which Nakajima called redemptive love.[29] He believed that a society where selfless love was practiced could resemble the Kingdom of God and that a society would grow toward such selfless love through the process of socialization.[30] Since for him the concept of "Christ" was equivalent to proper socialization, and since Jesus is the only person who fully manifested this "socialization", it is He who saves us from sin. The root of sin is selfish and egoistic motivation for social behavior, and salvation can only be realized through Jesus Christ by following his example of selfless love.[31]

Also, after World War II, Japan produced great theologians such as Kazoh Kitamori (1916–1998) who introduced the theology of the pain of God. He believed that the essence of the gospel lay in the redemptive pain and suffering of God and that human pain was symbolic of God's. Kitamori compared it with the concept of *tsurasa* from Japanese literature and classic Japanese Stage Drama.[32] The word *tsurasa* means to suffer, to commit suicide or to murder a loved one in order to save others from pain.[33] In Kitamori's eyes, God the Father suffered by sacrificing His Son in order to redeem humanity. This is *tsurasa* love: enduring pain for the sake of another.[34]

Kanzo Uchimura's Non-Church Movement *(mukyokai)* is one of the important contributions that Christianity has made to Japanese life. Uchimura believed that organizational church couldn't offer salvation. Rather, it comes only through belief in Christ. In his view, the church was not merely a building, but a living community of people. Many in the West, where post-modern thinking is now dominant, are now considering the ideas of *mukyokai*. Mullins considers the value of the Non-Church Movement to be beyond question. For him, it is the most widely known and respected expression of Japanese Christianity.[35] Because he was a prolific writer and Christian thinker, Uchimura was respected by many individuals both inside and outside Christian circles. Many of his disciples have likewise been well-known intellectual figures, authors, and university presidents.[36]

The Non-Church movement is well known for speaking out against social injustice. During 1930s and 1940s, they opposed Japanese nationalism and militarism. The Non-Church movement included a number of well-known personalities in the fields of

216

theology, arts and sociology, for example, Tadao Yanaihara, a prominent economist, and Shigeru Nanbara, a political scientist. Both became presidents of the University of Tokyo. Masao Sekine, Koki Nakazawa, Toraji Tsukamoto, a biblical scholar, and Saburo Takahashi are among well-known Japanese theologians.[37]

8.4 Contributions to Various Areas of Intellectual Life

Literature plays a significant role in Japanese culture and society. Japanese people enjoy reading novels. Some Christians are numbered among Japan's most prominent novelists.

According to Kaname Takado, by the end of 1945, there was not a single active Christian writer in Japan, but by 1970 there were over 20.[38] In Takado's assessment, Japanese Christian novelists not only struggle to be Christian, and remain so, in a society in which Christians are in the minority, but they also struggle to both be Japanese and preserve their reputation as authors. [39] Takado compares the Japanese Christian writers of post-World War II to a voice crying in the wilderness imbued with the hope of resurrection, freedom from the annihilating force of death.[40] Takado praises the significance of the country's Christian writers' overall contribution to Japanese society. Presently, the Japanese population, both Christian and non-Christian, reads the works of Japanese Christian authors. Their literary works transcend ideological and theological conflicts, overcome denominational barriers, and diminish perceived differences between Christian and non-Christian. For this reason they also provide an open forum for reading and dialogue.[41] One of the main contributions of Japanese Christian authors is that they

217

have produced a wealth of literature that articulates the Christian faith and thought in the indigenous idiom of the Japanese people and their daily life.[42]

Shusaku Endo (1923-1996) is one of the most well-known of Japanese writers in the West. At least seven of his novels are now available in translation. He is unusual among Japanese writers because of his frequent treatment of Christian themes.[43] His works are often historical in nature, such as *Chinmoku* (1966) (trans. *Silence* (1961)) and *Samurai* (1980) (trans. *The Samurai* (1982)). According to Napier, many of them deal with the miraculous within the framework of questions of faith. *Sukyandaru* (1986) (trans. *Scandal* (1988)) is perhaps the most explicitly 'fantastic' of all his writings.[44]

Endo, however, is not the only Christian writer in Japan. The appendix includes a list of Japanese Christian novelists. Among them are Rinzo Shiina (1911–1973), Yoshiro Ishihara (1915–1977), Arimasa Mori (1912–1976), Takehiko Fukunaga (1918–1979), Toshio Shimao (1917–1986), Sawako Ariyoshi (1913–1984), Kunio Ogawa (1927–2008), Ayako Sono (1931–), Shumon Miura (1926–), Hiro Sakato (1924–), Tomie Ohara (1912–2000), Takako Takahashi (1932–), Toshio Moriuchi (1936–), Otohiko Kaga (1929–), Komimasa Tanaka (1925–2000) and Ayako Miura (1922–1999). Almost every author on the list has won various prestigious awards for their work. A selected list of their books is also included in the appendix.

Makoto Fujimura is a well-known contemporary Christian artist, who is recognized worldwide as a cultural shaper. A presidential appointee to the National Council on the Arts from 2003-2009,

218

Fujimura served as an international advocate for the arts, speaking with decision makers and advising governmental policies on the arts.[45] Fujimura's work is exhibited at galleries around the world, including Dillon Gallery in New York, Sato Museum in Tokyo, The Contemporary Museum of Tokyo, Tokyo National University of Fine Arts Museum, Bentley Gallery in Arizona, Gallery Exit and Oxford House at Taikoo Place in Hong Kong, and Vienna's Belvedere Museum.[46]

Even though this chapter was not intended to be an extended report on the contribution of Christianity to the Japanese society and culture, it does, I believe, nevertheless make it clear that Christianity has indeed influenced Japan, specifically that it has contributed to the social and cultural development of this nation. It might not have acquired vast numbers of adherents, but its influence runs deeper than it may initially seem.

Notes

1   Edwin O. Reischauer, *The Japanese Today: Change and Continuity* (Cambridge: The Belknap Press of Harvard University Press, 1988), 213.

2   Ernest W. Clement, *Christianity in Modern Japan*. (Philadelphia American Baptist Publication Society, 1905), 26.

3   Sekiji Nishiyama, "The Christian Contribution to Japanese Education" *The Open Court*: Vol. 1911: Iss. 7, Article 6. (1911) http://opensiuc. lib.siu.edu/ocj/vol1911/iss7/6

4   Sally A. Hastings, "Gender and Sexuality in Modern Japan" in *A Companion To Japanese History*, ed. William M. Tsutsui (Oxford: Blackwell Publishing Ltd, 2007), 375.

5   Ibid.

6   Ibid.

7   Ibid.

8   Ibid.

9   Ibid.

10   Yuk Heung Li, *Woman's Education in Meiji Japan and Development of Christian Girls' School* (Hong Kong: University of Hong Kong, 1993).

11   John F. Howes, *Japan's Modern Prophet: Uchimura Kanzo, 1861-1930* (Vancouver: The University of British Columbia Press, 2005), 322.

12   Koichi Endo, "Christian Social Welfare and the Modernization of Japan," in *Handbook of Christianity in Japan*, ed. Mark R. Mullins (Leiden: Brill, 2003), 343.

13   Hastings, 375.

14   Ibid.

15   Hastings, 377.

16   "From the booklet "The History of Buraku Discrimination and
      the Catholic Church in Japan" at the 4th Symposium on the
      Bible and Discrimination was held at Kawara-Machi Church in
      Kyoto in September 1995. (Kyoto: Japan Catholic Committee
      for Buraku Issues).

17   Mark R. Mullins, "Christianity as a Transnational Social Movement:
      Kagawa Toyohiko and the Friends of Jesus" in *Japanese Religions*
      Vol. 32, No.1 & 2 (Kyoto: Center for the Study of Japanese
      Religions, 2007),71.

18   Operation Japan (OJ) is a resource available on CD-ROM. It
      was developed by *Reaching Japanese For Christ*. OJ contains
      relevant information about Christianity by prefecture in Japan.
      More information can be found at the website
      (http://www.rjcnetwork.org).

19   Ibid.

20   Ibid.

21   Carl Michelson, *Japanese Contributions to Christian Theology*
      (Philadelphia: Westminster Press, 1960), 9.

22   A selected list of Japanese theologians is provided in the appendix.

23   Yasuo Furuya, 48.

24   Furuya, 47.

25   Ibid.

26   Furuya, 51.

27   Ibid.

28   Ibid.

29   Charles Hugh Germany, *Protestant Theologies in Modern Japan: A History of Dominant Theological Currents From 1920-1960* (Tokyo : IISR Press, 1965), 74.

30   Germany, 73.

31   Furuya, 52.

32   Brinkman, 108.

33   Ibid.

34   Kazoh Kitamori, *The Theology of the Pain of God* (Richmond: Knox, 1965) 134-135.

35   Mullins 1998, 55.

36   Ibid.

37   Furuya,74.

38   Kaname Tadako, "Japanese Christian Writers," in *Christianity in Japan, 1971–90,* eds. Kumazawa Yoshinobu & David L. Swain (Tokyo: Kyo Bun Kwan aka The Christian Literature Society of Japan, 1991), 259.

39   Ibid.

40   Tadako, 260.

41   Tadako, 269.

42   Ibid.

43   Susan J. Napier, *The Fantastic in Modern Japanese Literature: The Subversion of Modernity* (London: Routledge, 1996), 239.

44   Ibid.

45   www.makotofujimura.com/bio

46   Ibid.

Why is **Christianity** Not Widely
Believed in Japan?

Chapter 9

FINAL REFLECTIONS

9.1 Summary

After the introduction in chapter one, I briefly outlined Japan's Christian history in chapter two. Chapter three discussed possible areas of conflict between the Japanese and Western Christian worldviews. The concept of *wa,* or harmony, was constantly referred to in that chapter. The Japanese are required to maintain social harmony at all costs, and any act that undermines this harmony is considered troublesome. Thus, becoming a devoted Christian can undermine *wa* in terms of various social, cultural, and religious responsibilities. If being converted to Christianity disturbs the overall social conduct of a Japanese person with respect to a given group, then Christianity will be suppressed either by that individual or by his or her environment. Further, in chapter three, I discussed some religious views of the Japanese and outlined the ways in which these contradict Western Christian views.

Chapter four reviewed theological concepts such as sin, life after death, ancestor veneration, and the exclusiveness of Christ from a Japanese cultural and religious perspective. I also examined theological factors that bear on the concept of *wa* and indicated that it promotes harmony between the existing mainstream religions in Japan: Shinto, Buddhism and Confucianism. In contradiction to this, Christianity does not promote harmony *per se* between itself and other religions. From a Japanese perspective, Christianity disturbs

225

the *wa* and promotes absolutism: an absolute God, an absolute path to salvation, an absolute church, and an absolute religion.

Chapter five focused on missiological factors associated with the attempt to Christianize Japan. I described the manner in which Christianity was introduced to the Japanese people throughout history. Some approaches to proselytize them collided with some aspects of Japanese culture and even with the moral and social commitments of some of native Japanese Christian thinkers. Missionaries who came to Japan claimed to preach a naked gospel and to offer a pure version of Christianity. However, they neglected to acknowledge the fact that their version of Christianity was influenced by Western and other cultures. They considered their own Christianity to be "absolute."

Chapter six discussed social factors such as family obligations and neighborhood duties along with occupational and educational participation of most Japanese people. I came to the conclusion that the average Japanese person may not have enough time and space to fully participate in a committed Christian life that demands intensive involvement.

In chapter seven, I outlined various factors in Japanese political life as they relate to Christianity and asked whether they have contributed to its lack of success in Japan. I provided a brief overview of them in a historical context, starting from the sixteenth century. It is my view that Western Christianity and the political views that accompany it have often, intentionally or otherwise, worked together to create problems for Christianity in non-Western countries. This is particularly evident in Japan. In the end, America

226

is seen as a conquering nation, the one that defeated Japan; Japan has been forced to develop a concept of itself as a vanquished nation that was defeated by America in World War II. No matter how stable the relationship between these two nations might be at this point in time, the religion of the occupier will often be linked to a dynamic of dominance.

Finally, chapter eight described some of Christianity's positive contributions to Japanese life with the aim of succinctly clarifying the further value that Christianity can have for Japanese culture. In chapter eight, I described the positions to which native Christians have risen in Japanese society—novelists, writers, human rights activists, and even some prime ministers.

9.2 Concluding Remarks

1. It is clear that the formation of a newly centralized Japanese political state in the sixteenth century, together with its 250 years of isolation from the West and Japan's political decision to ban missionary activities prevented the spread of Christianity during this period. Unlike some other colonized nations that had already been subdued by the Western powers and were in the process of being Christianized, Japan had the political capacity and the military power to block the intrusion of Western powers and their religion. This could be one of the reasons why there is not a higher percentage of Christians in Japan today. As said, it stands in sharp contrast to other colonized nations such as the Philippines or some West African countries (e.g., Ghana).

2. In the past, Christians were not culturally sensitive when it came to dealing with non-Western cultures and peoples. Contextualization of its message is a crucial point. The message ought to be conveyed in the language of the Japanese culture and within an appropriate social context. God's revelation and human culture are inseparable. Within Japanese culture there are commonalities that can be addressed and discussed. As M. A. C. Warren observes, God was already there before the Western missionaries came:

> A deep humility by which we remember that God has not left himself without witness in any nation at any time. When we approach the man of another faith than our own it will be in a spirit of expectancy to find how God has been speaking to him and what new understandings of the grace and love of God we may ourselves discover in this encounter. Our first task in approaching other people, another culture, another religion, is to take off our shoes, for the place we are approaching is holy. Else we may find ourselves treading on men's dreams. More serious still, we may forget that God was here before our arrival.[1]

3. It is decisive that Christians—indigenous and expatriate alike—attempt to find more and new ways of integrating Christianity and the religious culture of Japan, especially when it comes to ancestral veneration, important calendar dates for religious celebrations, funeral ceremonies, and other cultural events. After all, as history

228

makes clear, the same thing also happened during the early church era—Christianity integrated with a number of the cultural elements of each people group it converted.

Alternative theologies and interpretations of ancestor veneration and new thinking about the relation to the dead could possibly play a crucial role in reconfiguring Christianity in Japan. Martien Brinkman rightfully claims that, for instance, Protestant missionaries think that death results in an immediate separation, with a person going to either heaven and hell, and that after a relative dies it is too late for others to honor or pray for them.[2] He argues that for the majority of Japanese, this eternal separation from their ancestors is unacceptable.[3] Even the Jewish people remember their ancestors and call upon the God of Abraham, Isaac, and Jacob in doing so. Robert Lee rightfully suggests that missiological thinking points to the conclusion that contextualization is the way to introduce the Christian faith to the Japanese so that they can relate to it out of their own religious experience.[4] Understanding native religious experience, both individual and collective, can be the key to transferring the Christian message to the people of other cultures. This is especially true in Japan. With Robert Lee, I believe that Christian religious experience can be contextualized with respect to the Japanese religious heritage.[5] Jesus Christ also spoke in the cultural context of His time and He, too, adapted His message appropriately. Consider the fact that terms such as "kingdom," "Lamb of God," "good shepherd," "evangelism," "apostles", etc. were all borrowed from Jewish, Greek, Persian and Roman sources and came to be incorporated into the Christian message.

229

4. It is crucial that Christianity becomes more sensitive to the idea of harmony and collectivism in Japan. Often Western Christianity is strongly individualistic and that is a serious hindrance in Japan. Hence, in Japan Christianity might seek common ground with the Jewish concept of community and take distance from the identification with Western individualism. As noted, making a personal choice in any area of life is often not considered acceptable in Japan if disrupts harmony in the family, or if it undermines proper social conduct and leads to the abrogation of other responsibilities. Christians could try to find alternatives that enable new Japanese converts to live out their faith without being expelled from their neighborhood communities or families. Or, perhaps postmodern, stressful Japanese society could embrace a different form of Christianity. There might be a new way in which technology and social care are dealt with, if tradition and community are allowed to play an increasingly important role in its development there. Japan is an extremely stressful society, one in which everything moves rapidly. Still, in the midst of the ongoing pressure of affairs, the Japanese are looking for inner peace. Can the church offer alternatives to this stress, perhaps by relocating its facilities outside the city, by placing them in a natural setting with an authentic Japanese atmosphere, where people, both Christian and non-Christian, can go to enjoy nature and, at the same time, hear the Christian message? Perhaps it could be conveyed in a more Japanese environment with traditional music, in a communion service that is more like a tea ceremony? This may especially appeal to middle-aged and elderly people there.

5. I see possibilities for Christianity to raise public awareness

of the shortcomings of Japanese culture and challenge them. Every culture has its bright and dark sides. The light side is like the spirit of Christ and the dark side can be compared with the elements of evil. All cultures contain both of these elements. Contextualization means not only looking for the bright side, but also acknowledging the negative aspects of a culture. This is yet another aspect of contextualization. Stephen Bevans speaks of a praxis model for it, one that is informed by knowledge of the most intense level at which theology can operate, namely the level of reflective action discerning the meaning of the message, and contributing to the course of social change. It takes its inspiration neither from classic texts nor from classic behavior, but from present realities and future possibilities. The word 'praxis' derives from the Greek term for 'practice' or 'action'.[6] The praxis model requires reflecting on one's action in a given situation (e.g., experience, culture, social location, the social change to which one contributes and reading and re-reading of the Bible and various other Christian texts). These are brought to bear on one's present situation in order to bring about positive change through committed and intelligent action. In the case of Japan, biblical texts and theologies can be constantly reinterpreted and applied within a given context. Christianity can continue to promote spiritual transformation with an eye to encouraging social, economic, political change in Japan from a Christian perspective.

6. The Christian message should be a force for the edification of any culture. It must challenge and redefine its social context and call for a change in the hearts and minds of people, for conversion and radical transformation, both individual and collective. Bevans

231

takes such an approach to be prophetic in nature. It assumes that every context is the setting for reformation. It confronts 'the culture of death' with a gospel of light, as John Paul II stated.[7] As discussed in chapter eight, at the end of nineteenth century, Christianity stimulated existing feminist movements in Japan and so brought about improvements in women's conditions and rights. Yet, in most Western countries feminism was regarded as being opposed to various Christian traditions. This points to the conclusion that evangelistic efforts should not be defined in terms of, or limited by, the conditions of a given culture; instead they should change the culture so that it more clearly expresses the teachings of Christ. If they can do this, Christians will have found ways to bring the gospel to the heart of every Japanese.

7. Japanese Christianity itself has gone through periods of demographical decline. We may therefore need to redefine our understanding of Christianity and of the Japanese church as an organization. I am doubtful that, in its current form as an established organization with buildings, elders, deacons, and religious structures, it will be able to reach the Japanese people. Operation World (2010) states that:

> The impact of the Japanese Church is inadequate. The Church must turn from its insular, bunker mentality to engage with society. The government is not adequately solving the social ills confronting Japan; the transforming power of Christ, as expressed through a revived church, is an answer

not being adequately offered. There is, however, a
new emphasis on evangelism in many churches and
a willingness to try new paradigms of ministry.[8]

8. Japanese society is presently facing a variety of challenges,
thus Christianity has the opportunity to fit into society as a whole
and be part of them. According to Operation World (2010), young
people between the ages of 18 and 23 are those who are most open
to the message of the gospel. 85 percent of Japanese teenagers
wonder why they exist, while 11 percent wish they had never been
born.[9] Obviously, young people in Japan urgently need help. It is
wonderful when churches do develop innovative means of reaching
youth. Currently, younger missionaries use contemporary music,
gospel singing and other art forms to convey the Christian message
to Japanese youth. Also, websites, forums, and chatting services
are now being created to offer a friendly atmosphere and provide
assistance to many young people. Bibles are being translated into
cartoon format and *manga* (comic) books. There is, for example,
a well-known *manga* Bible called *Messiah*. In February 2008, the
first volume of the *manga* Bible, *Messiah* was published. It was the
result of a collaborative effort between the Japan Bible Society and
the New Life League Japan; they intend to publish five volumes of
biblical stories.[10] Further, Christianity could improve the manner in
which Japan supports the elderly, or offers educational services to
schoolchildren. The missionaries' teaching of English or other foreign
languages has often been effective for reaching young Japanese.

9. Constantly reminding Japan of its imperialistic past and neglecting to hold ourselves accountable for the atrocities committed by Western Christianity throughout its history may not help the cause of Christianity in Japan. Hiroshi Suzuki writes,

> The most of the history of evangelism to Japanese is for Japanese to meet the West. But I want the Westerners to meet Japanese and to know the work of God manifested in our history and people.[11]

There is no doubt that Japan has indeed shed much innocent blood and been guilty of many crimes against humanity. However, those who proclaimed peace and condemned any and all crimes against humanity have often themselves committed crimes against humanity (e.g., the eradication of the indigenous peoples in the Americas and Australia, and the centuries long slave trade from Africa that was carried out in the name of Christ and Christianity). Who can possibly justify killing or murder? And what about the two nuclear bombs that were dropped on Japan at the cost of hundreds of thousands of lives? Was this a crime? Any assessment of this has to also take into account of the fact that, for centuries, Nagasaki was a major center of Japanese Christianity. On the other hand, other nations in Asia have called upon the Japanese people to repent for their nation's wrongdoing. Some Christians even relate Japan's natural calamities to her past. These are harsh and seemingly unfair judgments which can only further inhibit the Japanese acceptance of Christianity.

As a culture and a nation, Japan is certainly about more than war crimes or past persecution of Christians. Both have definitely occurred but they have occurred in every culture, including Western nations. What crimes have the Japanese people committed that Western nations have not themselves committed? How can slavery or the shedding of innocent blood ever be justified by anyone? How can one justify using Christianity as a tool for eradicating indigenous cultures? As Suzuki writes, "Why don't American Christians review the relation with Native Americans while German Confession Churches and Japanese Churches made statements on atrocities during the World War II?"[12]

10. Japan has a centuries-long history of engagement with Christianity, so it cannot be argued that it is unknown. If this were not so, Japan would not have had so many Christian novelists, writers whose books are read widely — by both Christians and non-Christians. Thus, the majority of the Japanese people know at least a little about Christianity. Still, for some reason they remain silent about it. Could it be that they see the Christian message as being concordant with the historical atrocities that Western nations have perpetrated in the world? At the same time the Japanese are constantly told that they ought to repent for Japan's atrocities. Japanese culture is a culture of silence. This is a fact that is deserving of lengthy reflection. The individual is required to keep his or her own thoughts inside for the sake of the well-being of others.

I would argue that Christianity has penetrated the Japanese consciousness more deeply than many of that Western people might think. Could it be that the Japanese think that Western Christians

235

have historically not lived out the message of Christ? That they have not brought Christ's initial intentions of peace, love and reconciliation to full realization? Japanese Christianity may indeed have greater depths than Westerners might think.

11. What constitutes success when it comes to Christianity and evangelizing other nations? Western culture, especially capitalism, has long influenced American Christianity. Some aspects of American Christianity have become thoroughly commercialized, and success in mission work has been reduced to announcing church membership figures, conducting televangelism, and even involvement with the allure of material gain and prosperity. Western missionary endeavors are more often assessed primarily by means of statistical analysis. Such habits of thought have also been transferred to other non-Western countries where Christianity is rapidly growing (e.g., Africa, Latin America and some Asian countries). Some elite pastors own private jets and preach in fully packed stadiums. Certainly Christianity is growing in those parts of the world — at least numerically. At the same time and in these same parts of the world, poverty, corruption, crime, and all kinds of other forms of societal malaise are also expanding. In fact, the majority of the nations which were formerly colonized and Christianized do not actually belong to the developed world — they are still struggling economically and politically.

If we look at growth merely in numerical terms and define success in statistical terms, Christianity has not yet been particularly successful in Japan. However, if we define success in terms of something more than numbers (e.g., in terms of influence), then I

236

would claim that Christianity can be considered successful in the contexts in which it has exerted an influence.

Christianity in Japan has produced for the world, especially the Christian world, great personalities like Kanzo Uchimura (1861–1930), Masahisa Uemura (1861–1925), Shusaku Endo (1923–1996), Danjo Ebina (1866–1937), Yasuo Furuya (1926–), Kosuke Koyama (1929–2009), Kazoh Kitamori (1916–1998) and many more Christian thinkers and writers.[13] It has contributed to art, education, and philosophy; many universities in Japan have their roots in Christianity; gender equality and labor rights movements trace some of their roots to it as well. Thus, it is reasonable to generalize that it has also contributed to Japan's overall well-being. Indeed, I consider the combination of Japan and Christianity to be a tremendous gift to humanity as a whole and to the universal church in particular.

12. Lastly, it is worthwhile to acknowledge that Japan has also influenced Christianity. While an evangelical focus on numerical growth and cultural influence is important, Christian virtues cultivated in the social context of Japanese minorities are also to be appreciated. Japanese culture shaped its Christian thinkers, who, for their part, inspired not only Christians in Japan but also elsewhere. The legacy of Christians like Kanzo Uchimura, Shusaku Endo, and many other Japanese Christians whose names have been mentioned here, persists. And, they are not only children of Christ, but also offspring of Japan.

9.3 Conclusion

"What are the main factors why Christianity has not yet succeeded in Japan?" This was the central question of this dissertation. I have approached it by looking at Christianity from several different perspectives as they relate to Japanese life. These were identified as factors related to the Japanese worldview, and also to theological, missiological, societal, and political factors. Based on what has been said in previous chapters, I here conclude that Christianity's lack of quantitative success in Japan must be understood in context of all of these factors. I am inclined to consider the worldview factors as well as the political ones most relevant. The former is in the very center of my quest, in search of answers for the main question of this dissertation.

If I were asked to summarize the Japanese worldview in a single word, I would choose for wa, or harmony. As indicated in chapter three, *wa* is the invisible force behind Japanese worldview. It is about harmony, inclusivism, corporatism and balance between people, groups, nature, ancestors, gods and even religions. The individualism of Western culture stands in stark contrast to this. It even manifests itself in the Western Christian worldview; it is reflected in Western Christian theology: the absoluteness of God and religion with less, or almost no room at all for other religions (chapters four & five).

Secondly, political factors are hidden, and interwoven with worldview factors in this culture. The Eurocentric Christian worldview combined with the past political / colonial ambitions of the West have caused misunderstandings and led to persecutions

238

of Christians by the Japanese. The Western ignorance that underlies these skewed interpretations of historical and political events, both past and present, is notable. It does indeed make a negative impression on the Japanese people. The West speaks of moral values, Christianity, democracy and civilization, and accuses Japan of crimes against humanity and colonial aggression at the same time it overlooks its own crimes against mankind—especially those carried out in the name of God and Church.

On the other hand, politically, the Japanese did not consider the West as their master, but rather as their rival. In particular, from the end of nineteenth century to the end of World War II, the Japanese not only competed with the West in the areas of technology and science, but they also had rival political ambitions and colonial agendas. The West had its own religion, i.e. Christianity, through which it justified its various acts of aggression and program of colonialism, so Japan needed a religion, too, i.e. State Shinto, in order to compete. Political and military victors dictate which individuals become the heroes of war and which ones are labeled criminals, which acts of aggression are justified and which are defined as war crimes. In other words, historic outcomes are often dictated by the victors alone.

Political factors are also linked with theological and missiological ones. Often the political *Zeitgeist* of a particular era or period penetrates to the practice of theology and missionary work. For instance, during colonial times, the Western powers dominated the world, acting on the assumption that Christianity could make the so-called uncivilized peoples "civilized." This resulted in unequal master-servant relationships between the Western missionaries

239

and their subjects, as described in chapter five. If Christian theology and missionary work are linked to the political agenda of the West as it engages other countries–either as this has been done in the past, or as it is done today–this is almost guaranteed to produce negative effects where the reception of Christianity is concerned, and Japan is a case in point.

The Christian message can be more effective, when it does not allow itself to be influenced and used by the political *Zeitgeist* of their own nations. Christians should therefore not allow themselves to be used by politicians wielding political agendas and instruments of power. Any state, or any given nation that considers itself "chosen" by God is capable of harming and damaging others. Such a state is capable of using religion (be it Christianity, Islam, Judaism or State Shinto), as a means of dominating others. However, the Christian mission has to be conceived and carried out for the sake of Christianity only. In other words, Christians should not go with the flow of political ideas, but give priority to the teachings of Christ.

Lastly, in purely numerical terms, Christianity has not been successful in Japan. This is simply a reality. However, in the end, success understood in purely quantitative terms may not count for more than influence-oriented success. It is my sincere hope that this dissertation has contributed something positive to a better understanding of the complex relationship between Japan and Christianity.

Notes

1   Stephen B. Bevans, *Models of Contextual Theology* (New York: Orbis
    Books, 2002), 56. Bevans refers to M.A.C. Warren's preface to
    the seven books in the Christian Presence Series (London: SCM
    Press, 1959–1966).

2   Brinkman, 122.

3   Ibid.

4   Lee, 68.

5   Lee, 95.

6   Bevans, 71.

7   Bevans, 117-8.

8   Mandryk, 492.

9   Mandryk, 493.

10 "Japan Bible Society" last visited 23 April, 2013. http://www.bible.
    or.jp/e/manga.html

11 Suzuki, 2002.

12 Ibid.

13 A selected list of Japanese theologians and Christian novelists
    are given in the appendix.

Why is **Christianity** Not Widely
Believed in Japan?

BIBLIOGRAPHY

Akashi, Kiomasa. "Is there Really a Second Chance?" Book review, *Logos Ministries Blog*, 31 October, 2011: http://www.logos-ministries.org/blog/?p=2454.

Ama, Toshimaro. *Why Are the Japanese Non-Religious? Japanese Spirituality Being Non-Religious in a Religious Culture.* Lanham: University Press of America, 2005.

App, Urs. "Francis Xavier's Discovery of Japanese Buddhism: A Chapter in the European Discovery of Buddhism" (part 1: Before the Arrival in Japan, 1547–1549). *The Eastern Buddhist* Vol. xxx No.1 (1997).

Anderson, Gerald H. (ed.) *Asian Voices in Christian Theology.* New York: Orbis Books, 1976.

Ann, Harrington, M. *Japan's Hidden Christians.* Chicago: Loyola University Press, 1993.

Ballhatchet, Helen J. "The Modern Missionary Movement" in *Handbook of Christianity in Japan* ed. Mark R. Mullins. Leiden: Brill, 2003.

Batchourine, Alexei. "The Shinto Concept of Kami" Moscow State University, the Faculty of Philosophy http://trubnikovann.narod.ru/Bachessa.htm

Beasley W.G. *The Rise of Modern Japan.* London: Weidenfeld and Nicolson, 1990.

Bernard, Mary. *Japan's Martyr Church.* Exeter: Catholic Records Press, 1926.

Bevans, Stephen B. *Models of Contextual Theology.* New York: Orbis Books, 2002.

Boxer, C.R. *The Christian Century in Japan 1549–1650.* Manchester: Carcanet Press Limited, 1993.

Braw, Monica. "Discovering the Reasons for American Censorship of the Atomic Bomb in Japan." Lecture presented at 60th anniversary of the atomic bombings of Hiroshima and Nagasaki. Hiroshima University, 2005.

Breen, John. "Shinto and Christianity: A History of Conflict and Compromise" in *Handbook of Christianity in Japan*, ed. Mark R. Mullins. Leiden: Brill, 2003.

Brinkman, Martien E. *The Tragedy of Human Freedom: The Failure and Promise of the Christian Concept of Freedom in Western Culture.* Amsterdam: Rodopi B.V., 2003.

Brinkman, Martien E. *The Non-Western Jesus: Jesus as Bodhisattva, Avatara, Guru, Prophet, Ancestor or Healer?* Sheffield: Equinox Publishing, 2009.

Caldarola, Carlo. *Christianity: The Japanese Way.* Leiden: Brill, 1979.

Chandler, Paul Gordon. *Pilgrims of Christ on the Muslim Road: Exploring a New Path Between Two Faiths.* Lanham: Rowman & Littlefield Publishing Group, 2007.

Christal, Whelan, (Trans). *Tenchi Hajimari no Koto: Beginning of Heaven and Earth; the Sacred Book of Japan's Hidden Christians.* Honolulu: University of Hawaii Press, 1996.

Clement, Ernest W. *Christianity in Modern Japan.* Philadelphia: American Baptist Publication Society, 1905.

Clift, Peter "Uh Oh, What Now? I have to Conduct a Funeral!" Funerals as Wonderful Opportunities to Proclaim the Gospel of Hope in *The Unseen Face of Japan: Culturally Appropriate Communication of the Gospel.* Hayama Semina Annual Report, Tokyo (2001).

Dale, Kenneth. *Coping with Culture: The Current of the Japanese Church.* Tokyo: Lutheran Booklets, No. 3, 1996.

Davies, Roger and Ikeno, Osamu. *The Japanese Mind: Understanding Contemporary Japanese culture.* Boston: Tuttle Publishing, 2002.

De Leeuw, Paul. "Naka-Ima: Space in Japan." *The Netherlands-Japan Review:* Volume 2, nr.1, Spring (2011).

DeWitt, Richard. *Worldviews: An Introduction to the History and Philosophy of Science.* Chichester: Wiley-Blackwell: 2010.

Dower, John W. "Black Ships & Samurai: Commodore Perry and the Opening of Japan (1853–1854)", Visualizing Cultures, http://ocw.mit.edu/ans7870/21f/21f.027/black_ships_and_samurai/bss_essay02.html

Earhart, H.B. *Religions of Japan: Many Traditions Within One Sacred Way.* New York: Harper and Row, 1984.

Elison, George. *Deus Destroyed: The Image of Christianity in Early Modern Japan.* Massachusetts: Harvard University Asia Center, 1988.

Endo, Koichi. "Christian Social Welfare and the Modernization of Japan," in *Handbook of Christianity in Japan,* ed. Mark R. Mullins. Leiden: Brill, 2003.

Endo, Shusaku. *Silence.* New Jersey: Taplinger Publishing Company, 1980.

244

Eto, Jun. "The censorship operation in occupied Japan," in *Press Control Around the World,* ed. Jane Curry and Joan Dassin. New York, N.Y.: Praeger Publishers, 1982.

Flemming, Dean. *Contextualization in the New Testament: Patterns for Theology and Mission.* Downers Grove: Intervarsity Press, 2005.

Francis, Carolyn Bowen and Nakajima, John Masaaki. *Christians in Japan.* New York: Friendship Press Inc., 1991.

Fujiwara, Atsuyoshi. "Theology of culture in a Japanese context: a believers' church perspective." PhD diss., Durham University, 1999.

Fukuda, Mitsuo. *Developing A Contextualized Church As A Bridge to Christianity in Japan.* Gloucester: Wide Margin, 2012.

Furuya, Yasuo (ed.) *A History of Japanese Theology.* Grand Rapids: Wm. B. Eerdmans Publishing Co., 1997.

Germany, Charles Hugh. *Protestant Theologies in Modern Japan: A History of Dominant Theological Currents From 1920–1960.* Tokyo: IISR Press, 1965.

Hall, John Whitney. *Japan: Prehistory to Modern Times.* Frankfurt am Main: S. Fischer Verlag, 1991.

Hastings, Sally A. "Gender and Sexuality in Modern Japan" in *A Companion To Japanese History,* ed. William M. Tsutsui. Oxford: Blackwell Publishing Ltd, 2007.

Hays, Jeffrey. "Koreans in Japan: Discrimination, Citizenship, North Korean Schools and Japanese Wives in North Korea" in Facts & Details: http://factsanddetails.com/japan.php?itemid=635&catid=18, last modified in January 2013.

Hendry, Joy. *Understanding Japanese Society,* 3rd edition. London: Routledge Curzon, 2003.

Hiebert, P.G. "Critical Contextualization" in *Missiology: An International Review* 12(3), 1984.

Higashibaba, Ikuo. *Christianity in early modern Japan: Kirishitans belief and practice.* Leiden: Brill, 2001.

Hori, Ichiro. *Folk Religion in Japan: Continuity and Change.* Chicago: University of Chicago Press, 1968.

Howes, John F. *Japan's Modern Prophet: Uchimura Kanzo 1861–1930.* Vancouver: University of British Columbia, 2005.

Inagaki, Hisakazu and Jennings, J. Nelson. *Philosophical Theology and East-West Dialogue.* Amsterdam: Editions Rodopi B.V., 2000.

Inoue, Nobutaka. "Perspectives Towards Understanding the Concept of Kami," in *Contemporary Papers on Japanese Religions,* online version

(1988). http://www2.kokugakuin.ac.jp/ijcc/wp/cpjr/kami/inoue.
html#tnoteI

Inoue, Yoji. *The Faces of Jesus in Japan*. Tokyo: Nihon Kirisuto-Kyodan
Shuppankyi, 1994.

Ion, A. Hamish. "The Cross Under an Imperial Sun: Imperialism,
Nationalism, and Japanese Christianity, 1895–1945," in *Handbook of
Christianity in Japan*, ed. Mark R. Mullins (Leiden: Brill, 2003).

Jennings, J. Nelson *Theology in Japan: Takakura Tokutaro, 1885–1934*.
Lanham: University Press of America, 2005.

Joseph, Kenny. "Response to Peter Clift's presentation, Funerals as
Wonderful Opportunities" in *The Unseen Face of Japan: Culturally
Appropriate Communication of the Gospel*. Hayama Seminary Annual
Report, Tokyo (2001).

Kato, Naoko. *War Guilt and Postwar Japanese Education*. M.A. Thesis, The
University of British Colombia, 2002.

Kentaro, Miyazaki. "Hidden Christians in Contemporary Nagasaki."
Crossroads the Online Journal of Nagasaki History and culture: http://
www.uwosh.edu/home_pages/faculty_staff/earns/miyazaki.html

Kirby, Rob. "Is it a scandal that Gen. MacArthur thought Christianity would
help Japan?" *Beliefnet* accessed April 8, 2013. http://blog.beliefnet.
com/on_the_front_lines_of_the_culture_wars/2011/06/scandal-gen-
eral-douglas-macarthur-thought-christianity-would-help- japan.html

Kingston, Jeff. *Contemporary Japan: History, Politics, and Social Change
since 1980s*. West Sussex: Wiley-Blackwell, 2010.

Kishida, Shu. *A Place for Apology: War, Guilt and US-Japan Relations*.
Lanham: Hamilton Books, 2004.

Kishimoto, Hideo. *Reminiscences of Religion in Postwar Japan*. Tokyo:
Department of Religious Studies, Tokyo University, 1963.

Kitagawa, Joseph M. "The Contemporary Religious Situation in Japan,"
Japanese Religions II 2–3 (1961).

Kitamori, Kazoh. *The Theology of the Pain of God*. Richmond: Knox, 1965.

Kohls, Gary G. "The Bombing of Nagasaki August 9, 1945: The Untold
Story." http://www.lewrockwell.com/orig5/kohls8.html (August 6,
2007).

Kubo, Arimasa. "Salvation for the Dead, Second Chance Theology: Hades
is Not Hell." http://www2.biglobe.ne.jp/~remnant/hades.htm

Kumazawa Yoshinobu & David L. Swain. Tokyo: Kyo Bun Kwan aka The
Christian Literature Society of Japan, 1991.

Lande, Aasulv. *Meiji Protestantism in history and historiography*. Frankfurt
am Main: Verlag Peter Lang GmbH, 1989.

Leazer, Gary. "Shintoism," in *Center for Interfaith Studies' Bulletin*: (2010).

Lee, Robert. *The Clash of Civilizations: An Intrusive Gospel in Japanese Civilization*. Harrisburg: Trinity Press International, 1999.

Li, Yuk Heung. *Woman's Education in Meiji Japan and Development of Christian Girls' School*. Hong Kong: University of Hong Kong, 1993.

Lidin, Olof G. *Tanegashima: The Arrival of Europe in Japan*. Taylor & Francis e-Library, 2005.

Lewis, David "Questioning Assumptions About Japanese Society" Hayama Missionary Seminar Report 1988, PDF Version 1.1, November 2008.

Mandryk, Jason. *Operation World: The Definitive Prayer Guide to Every nation*, 7th edition. Colorado Springs: Biblica Publishing, 2010.

Masaaki, Shinya. "The Politico-Religious Dilemma of the Yasukuni Shrine in Religion and Politics in Present Day Japan" in *Politics and Religion Journal*: Volume IV, nr.1, Spring (2010), 41–55.

Mase-Hasegawa. Emi. *Christ in Japanese Culture: Theological Themes in Shusaku Endo's Literary Works*. Leiden: Brill, 2008.

Matsumoto, David. *The New Japan: Debunking Seven Cultural Stereotypes*. Yarmouth: Intercultural Press, Inc., 2002.

Michelson, Carl. *Japanese Contributions to Christian Theology*. Philadelphia: Westminster Press, 1960.

Mikio, Haruna. "MacArthur pondered Showa conversion." *Japan Times*. May 4, 2000, accessed April 8, 2013, http://www.japantimes.co.jp/news/2000/05/04/national/macarthur- pondered-showa-conversion/#.UWMkxL9GfjD.

Minagawa, John H. "Intercessors for Japan." *Pray For This Nation*. Newsletter may 11, 2003.

Miura, Hiroshi. *The Life and Thought of Kanzo Uchimura 1861–1930*. Cambridge: Wm B. Eerdmans, 1996.

Miyake, Noriyuki. *Belong, Experience, Believe: Pentecostal Mission Strategies for Japan*. Gloucester: Wide Margin, 2005.

Moni, Monir Hossain. "Christianity's Failure to Thrive in Today's Japan." Paper, Tokyo: Hitotsubashi University, Dept. of International and Asia-Pacific Studies, 2004.

Moriyuki, Abukuma (ed.) Daily Devotions with Uchimura Kanzo. Amsterdam: Foundation Press, 2010.

Mullins, Mark R. "Religion in Contemporary Japanese Lives," in *Routledge Handbook of Japanese Culture and Society*, ed. Victoria L. Bestor et al. London: Routledge, 2011.

Mullins, Mark R. Christianity as a Transnational Social Movement: Kagawa Toyohiko and the Friends of Jesus," *Japanese Religions*, Vol. 32, No. 1, 2007.

Mullins, Mark R. "The Social and Legal Status of Religious Minorities in Japan" paper presented at International Coalition for Religious Freedom Conference on "Religious Freedom and the New Millenium", Tokyo, Louisiana, May 23–25, 1998.

Mullins, Mark R. *Christianity Made in Japan: A Study of Indigenous Movements*. Honolulu: University of Hawai'i's Press, 1998.

Murayama-Cain, Yumi. "The Bible in Imperial Japan 1850 – 1950." PhD diss., University of St. Andrews, 2010.

Nagasawa, Makito. "Makuya Pentecostalism: A Survey" in *Asian Journal of Pentecostal Studies* 3/2 (2000).

Nakane, Chie. *Japanese Society*. California: University of California Press, 1973.

Napier, Susan J. *The Fantastic in Modern Japanese Literature: The Subversion of Modernity*. London: Routledge, 1996.

Nishi, Toshio. *Unconditional Democracy: Education and Politics in Occupied Japan, 1945–1952*. Stanford: Hoover Institution Press, 2004.

Nishiyama, Sekiji. "The Christian Contribution to Japanese Education." *The Open Court*: Vol. 1911: Issue. 7, Article 6, (1911).

Nobutaka, Inoue. "Perspectives Towards Understanding the Concept of Kami," in *Contemporary Papers on Japanese Religions* 4, 1988.

Noguchi, Tsuneki. "Religion and Its Relation to Politics in Japan and the United States". Translated from Noguchi Tsuneki (Professor Emeritus of Kogakkan University), "Nichi-Bei ryokoku ni okeru seiji to shukyo to no kankei" in Shinto Shukvo (Journal of Shinto Studies), no. 87 (April 1977), 17–31.

Oba, Nobutaka " 'I have no intention of discrimination, but . . . " – Toward a Sociology of Knowledge about Discrimination." Article, Monash University, 2013.

Obara, Shizuka. "The Yasukuni Issue: The process of the State Shinto and its contribution to the Yasukuni Shrine" paper, Decorah: Luther College, December 5, 2001.

Offner, Clark B. "A Foreign Christian's Struggle with Japanese Concepts of Respect, Honor, Veneration, Worship". Hayama Missionary Seminar Report 1988, PDF Version 1.1, November 2008.

Okano, Kaori H. "School Culture" in *The Cambridge Companion to Modern Japanese Culture*, ed. Yoshio Sugimoto. Port Melbourne: Cambridge University Press: 2009.

Okuyama, Minoru. "Japanese Challenges: Buddhism, Shintoism and Others" paper presented at *TOKYO 2010 Global Mission Consultation: From Edinburgh 1910 to Tokyo 2010.* May 13, 2010.

Palmer, Gary B. *Toward A Theory of Cultural Linguistics.* Austin: University of Texas Press, 1996.

Paramore, Kiri. *Ideology and Christianity In Japan.* Oxon: Routledge, 2009.

Parratt, John (ed). *An Introduction To Third World Theologies.* Cambridge: Cambridge University Press, 2004.

Perkin, Harold. *The Third Revolution: Professional Elites in the Modern World.* New York: Routledge, 1996.

Reader, Ian. *Religion In Contemporary Japan.* Honolulu: University of Hawaii Press, 1991.

Reid, David. *The Cultural Shaping of Japanese Christianity.* Berkeley: Asian Humanities Press, 1991.

Reischauer, Edwin O. *The Japanese Today: Change and Continuity.* Cambridge: The Belknap Press of Harvard University Press, 1988.

Reischauer, Edwin O. and Craig, Albert M. *Japan: Tradition & Transformation.* St. Leonards: Allen & Unwin Pty LTD, 1989.

Rohlen, Thomas P. *For harmony and strength: Japanese white-color organization in anthropological perspective.* Berkley: University of California Press, 1974.

Sansom, George B. *Japan: A Short Cultural History.* Stanford: Stanford University Press, 1978.

Schrimpf, Monika. "The Pro-and Anti-Christian Writings of Fukan Fabian (1565-1621)" In *Japanese Religions* Vol. 33, No.1 & 2. Kyoto: Center for the Study of Japanese Religions, July 2008.

Selden, Mark "Commemoration and Silence: Fifty Years of Remembering the Bomb in America and Japan," in *Living with the Bomb: American and Japanese Cultural Conflicts in the Nuclear Age,* ed. Laura Hein and Mark Selden. Armonk, NY: M.E. Sharpe, 1997.

Sherrill, Michael John. "Christian Churches in Post-War Japan" in *Handbook of Christianity in Japan.* Mark Mullins (Ed.). Leiden: Brill Academic Publishers, 2003.

Silberman, Bernard S. (ed.). *Japanese Character and Culture: A Book of Selected Readings.* Tucson: University of Arizona Press, 1962.

Storry, Richard. *A History of Modern Japan.* London: Penguin Books, 1990.

Sugimoto, Yoshio. *An Introduction to Japanese Society.* Cambridge: Cambridge University Press, 2003.

Suzuki, Hiroshi. "Why are Japanese Christians so few?" Paper presented as a seminar talk at the staff meeting of International Friendships Incorporation in Columbus, Ohio on June 26, 2002.

Tadako, Kaname. "Japanese Christian Writers," in *Christianity in Japan, 1971–90*, eds. Kumazawa Yoshinobu & David L. Swain. Tokyo: Kyo Bun Kwan aka The Christian Literature Society of Japan, 1991.

Takizawa, Nobuhiko. "Religion and the State in Japan," in *Readings on Church and State*, ed. James E. Wood, Jr. Waco, TX: J. M. Dawson Institute of Church-State Studies, 1989.

Takimoto, Jun *The Day The Lord Arose: How One Japanese Church was Led Into Spiritual Warfare*. Aichi: Praise Publications, 2007.

Tamaru, Noriyoshi and Reid, David (Eds.). *Religion in Japanese Culture: Where Living Traditions Meet a Changing World*. New York: Kodansha International, 1996.

Tsuneki, Noguchi. "Religion and Its Relation to Politics in Japan and the United States", 34. Translated from Noguchi Tsuneki (Professor Emeritus of Kogakkan University), "Nichi-Bei ryokoku ni okeru seiji to shukyo to no kankei" in Shinto Shukvo (Journal of Shinto Studies), no. 87 (April 1977), 17–31.

Turnbull, Stephen. *The Kakure Kirishitan of Japan: A Study of their Development, Beliefs and Rituals to the Present Day*. Richmond: Japan Library, 1988.

Uemura, Toshifumi. "The Way to State Shinto: In Comparison with Shrine Shinto." *The Unseen Face of Japan: Culturally Appropriate Communication of the Gospel*, ed. Cynthia Dufty. Tokyo: Hayama Missionary Seminar Report, 1988.

Yamauchi, Tomosaburo. "Some Aspects of Humanism that Combines East and West: MacArthur, Showa Tenno, and Justice Pal." *Bulletin of Osaka Kyoiku University*, Vol.61 No.2, 75–89. February 13, 2013.

Yoshimasa, Ikegami. "Holiness, Pentecostal, and Charismatic Movements in Modern Japan," in *Handbook of Christianity in Japan*, ed. Mark R. Mullins. Leiden: Brill, 2003.

Vu, Michelle A. "Mission Leader: Why So Few Christians in Japan?" *Christian Post Reporter*, May 18, 2010. http://www.christianpost.com/news/mission- leaderwhy-so-few-christians-in-japan-45217/

Why is **Christianity** Not Widely
Believed in Japan?

Why is **Christianity** Not Widely
Believed in Japan?

APPENDIX

Appendix I. A selected list of some Japanese Theologians & Christian Thinkers (Source: Yasuo Furuya (ed.), A History of Japanese Theology. Grand Rapids: Wm. B. Eerdmans Publishing Co., 1997 & other miscellaneous sources. The surnames are in bold.

Name	Orientation	Important Publications
Akaiwa, Sakae (1903– ?)	Dialectical Theology (Barthian) After the capitulation, he came to sympathize with Marxism more and more. In 1949 he declared his intention to join the Communist party, but he did not act on it. He eventually left Christianity	- Exodus from Christianity
Arai, Sasagu (1930–	Arai was a pioneer of the studies of Gnosticism after the discovery of the Nag Hammadi library.	- Early Christianity and Gnosticism (1971) - Jesus and His Age (1974) - New Testament and Gnosticism (1986) - Evangelium According to Thomas (1994) - Nag Hammadi Library ed. (4 vol.), (1997–1998) - Jesus Christ, Part1, Part2 (2001) - Collected Works of Arai Sasagu (10 vol. and addendum book), (June 2001–June 2002)

Appendix I. (*Continued*)

Name	Orientation	Important Publications
Asano, Junichi (1899–1982)	German influence	- A Study of the Prophets (1931) - Interpretation of some Psalms (1933) - Some Problems of the Old Testament Theology (1941) - A Study of the Israelite Prophets (1955) - A Study of the Book of Job (1962) - Commentary on the Book of Job (4 Vol.) 1965–1975
Ashida, Keiji (1867–1936)	Dialectical Theology (Barthian). He was one of leaders of a group of theologians to translate Barth's *Römerbrief*	- *Nihonteki Kirisutokyo* (Christianity on Japanese terms)
Doi, Masatoshi	More contextual in the sense that he emphasized on the meaning and experience of the individual believer.	- Theology of Meaning (1963)
Ebina, Danjo (1866–1937)	Christian – Shinto dialogue. He believed Christianity is universal religion and compatible with Shinto or Confucianism.	- *Reikai Shincho* "The Evangelization of Japan Viewed in its Intellectual Aspects" in Harvard Theological Review Vol. 2, No.2, April 1909. - The New Man
Fukuda, Masatoshi	Dialectical Theology (Barthian)	- Ordo Gratiae
Furuya, Yasuo (1926–)	Produced many studies of American Christianity He was interested in the relationship between Christianity and other religions	- Theology of Religions (1985)

Appendix I. (*Continued*)

Name	Orientation	Important Publications
Hatano, Seiichi (1877–1950)	He was known for his work in the philosophy of religion dealing mostly with eastern religion but also western philosophical thoughts in theological aspects of Christianity.	- Origin of Christianity (1908) - The Essence and Basic Problems of the Philosophy of Religion (1920) - Introduction to the Philosophy of Religion (1940)
Hino, Masumi (1874–1943)	Historical Christianity	- History of Christian Doctrine (1903) - Experimental Christianity (1907)
Hatano, Seiichi (1877–1950)	He was known for his work in the philosophy of religion dealing mostly with eastern religion but also western philosophical thoughts in theological aspects of Christianity.	- Origin of Christianity (1908) - The Essence and Basic Problems of the Philosophy of Religion (1920) - Introduction to the Philosophy of Religion (1940)
Hino, Masumi (1874–1943)	Historical Christianity	- History of Christian Doctrine (1903) - Experimental Christianity (1907)
Gordon, Hirabayashi (1918–2012)	Non-Church, Quaker American sociologist best known for his principled resistance to the Japanese American internment during World War II, and the court case which bears his name, *Hirabayashi v. United States*.	
Imai, Toshimichi	Old Testament Scholar	- Old Testament Theology (1911)
Inoue, Yohji	Catholic priest	- Japan and Jesus' Face (1976)
Ishida, Tomoo	Old Testament Scholar	- Co-published monograph series in *Zeitschrift fur die Alttestamentische* (1970s)

255

Appendix I. (*Continued*)

Name	Orientation	Important Publications
Ishihara, Ken (1887–1976)	Historical Theology	- The Philosophy of Religion (1916) - History of Christianity (1934) - The Source of Christianity (1972) - The Development of Christianity (1972) - Schleiermachers Reden über die Religion (1922)
Ishii, Jiro (1910–1987)	Opposed Barthian theology. Theology is not from subjectivism but from a Höhere Realismus	- A Study of Schleiermacher (1948)
Iwashita, Soichi (1889–1949)	Roman Catholics	- The Deposit of Faith (1941) - The History of the History of Medieval Philosophy - Medieval Currents of Thoughts (1928) - Neo-Scholastic Philosophy (1932) - Augustine's "City of God" (1935)
Kagawa, Toyohiko (1888–1960)	Social Gospel	- A Grain of Wheat - Love, the Law of Life (1929) - Brotherhood of Economics (1936)
Kan, Enkichi (1895–1972)	Social Gospel Gradually he became a Barthian	- Religious Revival (1934) - Modern Philosophy of Religion (1934) - The Turning of Christianity and its Principles (1930) - A Study of Carl Barth (1968) - A Study of Theology of Barth (1979) - Reason & Revelation (1953)
Kashiwai, En	Historical Theology	- Short History of Christianity (1909)
Kida, Kenichi	Old Testament Scholar	- Israelite Prophets: Their Duty and Writings
Kitamori, Kazoh (1916–1998)	Opposed Barthian theology. God of love suffers pain...	- The Theology of the Pain of God (1946)

256

Appendix I. (*Continued*)

Name	Orientation	Important Publications
Kimura, Yonetaro (1889–1949)	Dialectical Theology (Barthian)	- "A Survey of Thought Movements in 1932" in Japan Christian Yearbook 1933
Kohata, Fujiko	Old Testament Scholar	- Jahwist und Priesterschrift in Exodus 3 – 14 (1986)
Kozaki, Hiromichi (1856–1928)	Christian – Confucian dialogue	- *Seikyō Shinron* (1886) A New Study of Relation between Religion and Politics"
Kumano, Yoshikata	Dialectical Theology (Barthian)	- Introduction to Dialectical Theology (1932) - Journal New Weekly Evangelist. - Basic Questions of Christology (1934) - A study of the Johannine Epistles (1934) - Contemporary Theology (1934)
Matsutani, Yoshinori	Dialectical Theology (Barthian)	- Thinking of Theological Man - Introduction to the Doctrine of Trinity
Maeda, Goro		
Miyamoto, Takenosuke (1905–)	Influenced by Karl Barth and Takakura Tokutaro	- The Basic Problems of Christian Ethics (1939) - The Philosophy of Religion (1942) - Philosophy as Symbol (1948) - The Logic of the Religious Life (1949) - The Image of Man in Modern Christianity (1958) - Seiichi Hatano (1965) - The Basic Problems of the Philosophy of Religion (1968)
Morita, Yuzaburo	Human Rights, Peace, Philosophy	- Modernity of Christianity (1973)
Murata, Tsutomu	Historical Theology	- History of Reformation (1909)
Muto, Kazuo (1913–1995)	Influenced by Kierkegaard	- Between the Theology and Philosophy (1961)

Appendix I. (*Continued*)

Name	Orientation	Important Publications
Nakajima, Shigeru (1888–1946)	Social Gospel (National alliance of Social Christianity) Redemptive love (influenced by Kagawa)	- Magazine : Social Christianity - God and Community (1929) - Social Christianity & New Experience of God (1931) - The Essence of Social Christianity: The Religion of Redemptive Love (1937)
Nakazawa, Koki	Old Testament Scholar	- Studies of Deutro-Isaiah (1963)
Nakazawa, Koki	Non-Church/Biblical scholar	
Namiki, Koichi	Old Testament Scholar Weberian influences	- Ancient Israel and Its Surroundings (1979)
Nanbara, Shigeru	Non-Church Political scientist / President of University of Tokyo	
Nishimura, Toshiaki	Old Testament Scholar	- Prophesy and Wisdom in the Old Testament (1981)
Noro, Yoshio	Existential Theology	- Existential Theology (1964)
Odagaki, Masaya	Philosophy of Religion	- Openness of Christology?: A Study of the Relation Between the Historical Jesus and the Kerygmatic Christ (1969)
Odagiri, Nobou (1909–)	A layman Christian, medical doctor. The naive questions in his book attracted the interest of many Christians in Japan… He denied the deity of Jesus.	- The Mediator in the Bible: Problems in the Chalcedon Creed (1960)
Oga, Ichiro	Non – Church Botanist	
Ogawa, Keiji (1927–2012)	Barthian	- Subjectivity and Transcendence (1975)

258

Appendix I. (*Continued*)

Name	Orientation	Important Publications
Ohki, Hideo (1928–)	First who introduced Covenant Theology & Puritanism' idea on natural right to Japanese Christianity. Influenced by Brunner & Reinhold Niebuhr	- Theology of Japan (1989)
Otsuka, Setsuji (1887–1977)	Systematic Theology	- Prolegomena to Christian Ethics (1935) - Christian Anthropology (1948) - Outline of Christianity (1971)
Sakon, Kioshi	Old Testament Scholar	- Studies on Pslams (1972)
Sato, Shigehigo (1887–1935)	Introduced Luther to Japan Sato was critical to dialectic theology	- Young Luther (1920) - A Study of Religion of Experience (1924) - Luther's Basic Thoughts on Romans (1933)
Sato, Toshio (1923–)	Influenced by Karl Barth	- Modern Theology (1964)
Sekine, Masao	Great influence in Japanese Christendom A Leader of Mukyokai Influenced by Kyoto School of Religion He was influenced by emptiness concept in Buddhism.	- Studies on Duetero-Isaiah (1963) - Studies on the Psalms (1972)
Soyano, Teruo (1889–1927)	Philosophy Devoted to the studies of St. Augustine	- *Sei Augusutinusu no kenkyū*
Suzuki, Yoshihide	Old Testament Scholar	- Philosophical Studies on Deuteronomy (1987)
Tagaki, Mizutaro	Systematic Theology	- Great Dictionary of Christianity (1911)
Tagawa, Kenzo	New Testament Bible Scholar	- The New Testament As A Book (1997)
Takahashi, Saburo	Non-church movement	

Appendix I. (*Continued*)

Name	Orientation	Important Publications
Takakura, Tokutaro (1885–1934)	Evangelical; introduced Calvin to Japan	- Evangelical Christianity (1924) - Kingdom of Grace (1921) - Grace & Faithfulness (1921) - Grace & Calling (1925)
Takizawa, Katsumi (1906–1984)	Dialogue between Buddhism & Christianity Also influenced by Kitaro Nishida (1870–1945) He viewed Buddhism as a sister religion to Christianity	- Buddhism and Christianity
Teshima, Ikuro (1910–1973)	Non-Church, Pentecostal	- Introduction to the Original Gospel Faith. - The Love of the Holy Spirit. Tokyo: Makuya Bible Seminary. - The Jews and the Japanese: The Successful Outsiders.
Tominaga, Tokumaro	New Testament Scholar	- New Interpretation of Christianity (1909)
Tominomori, Kyoji (1887–1954)	A New Testament Scholar	- The Mythological Imagery in the Book of Revelation (1921)
Tsukamoto, Toraji (1885–1973)	Mukyokai Got Independent from Kanzo in 1929 Independent evangelist	- Monthly Journal: Bible Knowledge - Journal: Colloquial Translation of the New Testament - Paperback series: A Table of the Differences in the Gospel (1951)
Tsukimoto, Akio	Old Testament Scholar History of Religion, Assyriology	- Studies on the Mortuary in Ancient Mesopotamia (Ancient Orient and Old Testament) (1985)
Uchida, Yoshiaki	Old Testament Scholar Weberian influences	- Translated Max Weber's book *Das Antike Jutendum* into Japanese from 1962–1964

Appendix I. (*Continued*)

Name	Orientation	Important Publications
Uchimura, Kanzo (1861–1930)	Non Church Movement	- How I Became a Christian; Out of My Diary (1895) - The Diary of a Japanese Convert (1893) - Japan and the Japanese (1894) - Representative Men of Japan: Essays (1908)
Uemura, Masahisa (1857–1925)	Presbyterian Pastor, Translated the Old Testament and helped establish Meiji Gakuin University	- Hymns and Songs of Praise (1890) - He published several Christian Magazines such as The Magazine of The Universe (*Rikuggo Zasshi*) or On the Only Truth (*Shinri Ippan*) and a Weekly Christian Magazine called *Fukuin Shinpo*
Uoki, Tadakazu (1882–1954)	Luther & Calvin German Influence	- Protestant Theological Thoughts (1934) - Christian Spiritual History: The Spirit of Calvin's Theology (1948) - The Spiritual Tradition of Japanese Christianity (1941)
Watanabe, Zenda (1885–1978)	Systematic Theology	- The Theology of Old Testament Books (1921–24) - Introduction to five books of Moses (1949) - Before the Exodus (1972) - Canonicity of the Bible (1949) - Interpretation of the Bible (1954) - Theology of the Bible (1963)
Yagi, Seiichi	Dialogue between Buddhism & Christianity	- A Bridge to Buddhist Christian Dialogue (1990) - Falsehood of Ego and Religion (1980) - Jesus and Christ (1969) - Paul/Shinran Jesus/Zen (1969)

261

Appendix I. (*Continued*)

Name	Orientation	Important Publications
Yamamoto, Kano	Dialectical Theology (Barthian)	- Journal : Theology of the Cross - Politics & Religion——How did Barth Fight (1947) - Theology of Heilsgeschichte (1972)
Yamaya, Seigo (1889–1982)	New Testament Scholar	- The Theology of Paul (1936) - The New Testament: A New Translation and Exegesis (5 Vols. 1930–48) - The Origin of Christianity (2 vols. 1957–58) - Explanatory Bibliography of the New Testament (1943)
Yanaihara, Tadao	Non-Church Economist/President of University of Tokyo	- Religion and Democracy in Modern Japan (1948) - The Uniqueness of Christianity (1937) - Faith & Reality (1941) - The Faith of the Apostle Paul (1941) - The Outline of Christianity (1947) - The Essence of Christianity (1947) - Martin Luther (1947) - Synoptic Gospels (1952) - Introduction to Christian Ethics (1960) - History of Japanese Theological Thoughts (1968) - A History of Japanese Ethical Thoughts (article in the journal Gospel & The World)
Yoshimitsu, Yoshihiko (1904–1945)	Roman Catholics	- Catholicism, Thomas, Newman (1934)
Yoshimura, Yoshio	Dialectical Theology (Barthian) also interested in Kierkegaard	- Translated Barth's Commentary on Romans

Appendix II. List of Japanese Christian Novelists (Source: various, including Wikipedia)

Name of the Author	Important Publications	Notes
Ariyoshi, Sawako (1931–1984)	- Folksongs (1956) - The Wife of Hanaoka Seishu (1966) - Without Color (1964)	Nominated for Akutagawa prize His novels center on questions of social justice
Endo, Shusaku (1923–1996)	- Silence (1966) - Beside the Dead Sea (1973) - A Life of Jesus (1973) - Samurai (1980) - Scandal (1986)	Japan's best known novelist President of Japan's Pen Club
Fukunaga, Takehiko (1918–1979)	- Flowers (1954) - Rivers of Oblivion (1964) - Island of Death (1971)	Japan Literature Awards
Miura, Shumon (1926–)	- The Tower of Babel (1971) - Sacrifice (1972) - Indians of Musashino Plains, (1982)	Husband of Sono Ayano Former director of the Association of Japanese Writers
Miura, Ayako (1922–1999)	- *Hyōten (Asahi Shinbunsha, 1965). Translated into English as Freezing Point (Dawn Press, 1986).* - *Shiokari Tōge (Shinchōsha, 1968). Translated into English as Shiokari Pass (OMF Press, 1974).* - *Yuki no Arubamu (Shōgakkan, 1986). Translated into English as A Heart of Winter (OMF Press, 1991).* - *Kairei (Asahi Shinbunsha, 1981). Translated into English as Hidden Ranges (Dawn Press, 1993).* - *Hosokawa Garasha Fujin (Shufunotomosha, 1975). Translated into English as Lady Gracia (IBC Publishing, 2004).*	The themes she explores in her novels are primarily Biblical themes: human depravity and egoism on the one hand, and sacrifice and forgiveness of sin on the other. She is often compared and contrasted with the Japanese Catholic novelist Endo Shusaku, who lived around the same time.

Appendix II. (*Continued*)

Name of the Author	Important Publications	Notes
	- *Michi Ariki (Shufunotomosha, 1969). Translated into English as The Wind is Howling (Intervarsity Press, 1977)*	
Mori, Arimasa (1912–1976)	- On the Banks of River Babylon (1957) - Faraway Notre Dame (1967) - In Earthen Vessels - Light & Darkness - A Life of Abraham	Essayist influenced by Descartes, Pascal and Dostoevsky, Jean Paul Sartre and Maurice Merleau-Ponty
Ogawa, Kunio (1927–2008)	- A Certain Bible (1973) - That Man, *(referring to Judas)* - Songs of the King (1988)	He wrote about biblical Characters like Judas and David.
Ohara, Tomie (She) (1912–2000)	- A Woman Called En	In 1956, she received Women's Literature Prize for *Sutomai tsumbo* and 1960, the Mainichi Cultural Prize for Literature and Art for *Utsukushi to iu onna* and the Noma Literary Prize for *A Woman Called En.*
Shiina, Rinzo (1911–1973)	- Encounter (1952) - Beautiful Woman (1955) Confessions of a Prisoner (1969)	Influenced by Dostoevsky Winner of Literature Prize Ministry of Education (1955) Rinzo led a Christian Writers group called "Seed Group" and encouraged young authors like Abe Mitsuko and Mori Reiko
Sono, Ayako (1931–)	- Nameless Monument (1969) - Showers for the earth (1976) - God's defiled hand (1979) - His name is Joshua (1980) - Lamentations *(this novel is about the genocide in Rwanda..)*	She won the Akutagawa prize 1954 She presently (??) works as the president (JOMAS: Japan Overseas Missionaries Assistance Society)

Appendix II. *(Continued)*

Name of the Author	Important Publications	Notes
Takahashi, Takako (1932–)	- *Lonely Woman*, translated by Maryellen Toman Mori (New York: Columbia University Press, 2004). ISBN 978-0-231-13126-1. - "Congruent Figures" (*Sōjikei*), in *Japanese Women Writers: Twentieth Century Short Fiction*, translated by Noriko Mizuta Lippit and Kyoko Iriye Selden (Armonk, NY: M.E. Sharpe, 1991) - "Doll Love" (*Ningyō ai*), translated by Mona Nagai and Yukiko Tanaka in *This Kind of Woman: Ten Stories by Japanese Women Writers, 1960–1976*, ed. Yukiko Tanaka and Elizabeth Hanson (Stanford: Stanford University Press, 1982), 197–223. - "Holy Terror" (*Kodomo-sama*) and "A Boundless Void" (*Byōbo*), translated by Amanda Seaman in *The Massachusetts Review* 51/3 (Fall 2010): 439–55 and 456–81.	Takahashi received the 1985 Yomiuri Prize for *Ikari no ko* (Child of Wrath).
Kaga, Otohiko (1926–)	- *Kaerazaru natsu* (帰らざる夏, A Summer Long Gone) - *Shitsugen* (The Marsh) - *Furandoru no fuyu* (Winter in Flanders)	1968 Minister of Education Award for New Artists for *Furandoru no fuyu* (Winter in Flanders) 1974 Tanizaki Prize for *Kaerazaru natsu* (帰らざる夏, A Summer Long Gone) 1979 Japan Literature Grand Prize for *Senkoku* (The Verdict) 1985 Osaragi Jiro Prize for *Shitsugen* (The Marsh) 2011 Person of Cultural Merit

Appendix II.   (*Continued*)

Name of the Author	Important Publications	Notes
Tanaka, Komisama (1926–)	- *Rōkyoku shiasahimaru no hanashi/Mimi no koto* (浪曲師朝日丸の話/ミミのこと)	1979 Naoki Prize for *Rōkyoku shiasahimaru no hanashi / Mimi no koto* (浪曲師朝日丸の話/ミミのこと) 1979 Tanizaki Prize for *Poroporo* (ポロポロ)
Moriuchi, Toshio (1936–1990)	- *Hyoga ga kuru made ni.*	Yomiuri Prize for *Hyoga ga kuru made ni.*
Ayako, Miura (She) (1922–1999)	- Her novel, *Freezing Point*, was awarded top prize in a prestigious contest, and she went on to publish many bestsellers. - *Hyōten* (Asahi Shinbunsha, 1965). Translated into English as *Freezing Point* (Dawn Press, 1986). - *Shiokari Tōge* (Shinchōsha, 1968). Translated into English as *Shiokari Pass* (OMF Press, 1974). - *Yuki no Arubamu* (Shōgakkan, 1986). Translated into English as *A Heart of Winter* (OMF Press, 1991). - *Kairei* (Asahi Shinbunsha, 1981). Translated into English as *Hidden Ranges* (Dawn Press, 1993). - *Hosokawa Garasha Fujin* (Shufunotomosha, 1975). Translated into English as *Lady Gracia* (IBC Publishing, 2004). - *Michi Ariki* (Shufunotomosha, 1969). Translated into English as *The Wind is Howling* (Intervarsity Press, 1977)	The themes she explores in her novels are primarily Biblical themes: human depravity and egoism on the one hand, and sacrifice and forgiveness of sin on the other. She is often compared and contrasted with the Japanese Catholic novelist Endo Shusaku, who lived around the same time.

Why is **Christianity** Not Widely
Believed in Japan?

Why is **Christianity** Not Widely
Believed in Japan?

ABOUT THE AUTHOR

Samuel C. Lee is president of Foundation University Amsterdam. He also lectures sociology and contextual theology. Lee holds M.A. degree in Sociology of Non Western Societies / Development Sociology (Leiden University) and PhD in Intercultural Theology (VU University / Free University Amsterdam). His research areas are Japanese culture & society, Christianity in Japan, sociology of religion and contextual theology. Samuel Lee is member of Japan Evangelical Missionary Association (JEMA) and member of the steering committee of National Synod Netherlands (NatSyn).

ti

CPSIA information can be obtained at www.ICGtesting.com
Printed in the USA
BVOW02s2253240316

441458BV00011B/205/P